Easy Dips

Using Herbs

112 Dip Recipes plus

42 Ethnic Dips From Around The World

Most Using Fresh Or Dried Herbs

Published by

Long Creek Herbs

P.O. Box 127

Blue Eye, MO 65611

417-779-5450

Lcherbs@interlinc.net

www.Longcreekherbs.com

ISBN 1-889791-21-0

Introduction

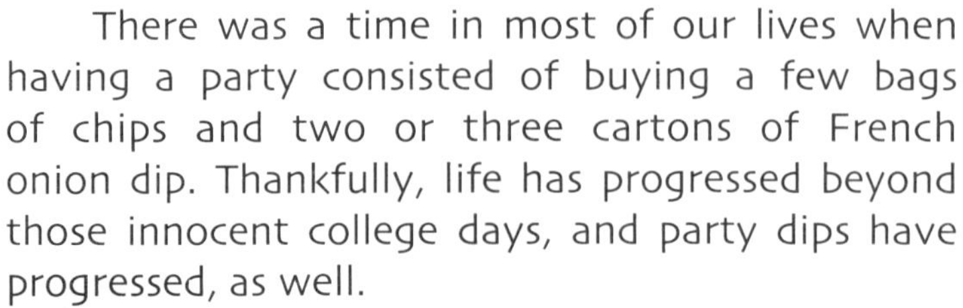

There was a time in most of our lives when having a party consisted of buying a few bags of chips and two or three cartons of French onion dip. Thankfully, life has progressed beyond those innocent college days, and party dips have progressed, as well.

Many of the recipes in this book include either fresh or dry herbs. Use fresh if you can, the flavor is better. The dips are easy to make and taste so much better than the store-bought ones. If you're adventurous, you'll find lots of exotic, ethnic dip recipes from around the world. The more adventurous you are, the more you will find in this book. But if you want to keep things simple, you will also find plenty of recipes to keep you happy.

Entertaining and or having a party, can still be easy, quick and simple and the recipes that follow can help. Enjoy entertaining your friends!

Jim Long

For those who wish to grow their own fresh herbs see the sources page in the back of this book.

Avocado Dip, Creamy

A simple, quick to make dip that's good with tortilla chips, raw vegetables or crackers.

3 ripe avocados, peeled, pitted
2 cups sour cream
2 ripe Roma tomatoes
3 green onions, cut in pieces
Juice of 1 fresh lime
1/2 teaspoon hot sauce

• Cut Roma tomatoes in half, gently squeeze out some of the seed and juice. Put tomatoes and rest of ingredients in blender and blend until smooth.

• Makes about 3 1/2 cups.

Baked Onion Dip

Serve this with sturdy crackers, corn chip "scoops" or toasts.

2 cups shredded cheddar cheese
2 cups mayonnaise
2 cups chopped sweet onion
1 teaspoon hot sauce
1/2 teaspoon Worcestershire sauce
Dash black pepper and salt
2 tablespoons grated Parmesan cheese

• Preheat oven to 325°F. Combine ingredients except Parmesan cheese and pour into lightly greased baking dish. Bake for about 25 minutes until dip is lightly browned and onions are tender. Top with Parmesan cheese and serve hot.

• Makes about 6 cups.

Balsamic Tomato Dip

Balsamic vinegar gives this dip its personality. Serve it with chips, crackers or your favorite dippers.

1 15-ounce container ricotta cheese
1/2 cup grated Parmesan cheese
2 tablespoons drained, chopped sun-dried tomatoes
1 tablespoon balsamic vinegar
2 green onions, diced fine
1 tablespoon chopped fresh parsley

• Put everything except onions and parsley in a food processor and process. Pour into serving bowl and mix in diced green onions. Top with 1 tablespoon chopped fresh parsley. Refrigerate until ready to serve.

• Makes about 1 3/4 cups.

Barbecue Dip for Chicken

Serve this dip with buffalo chicken wings or grilled chicken wings.

1/2 cup brown sugar
2 cups catsup
1 cup prepared mustard
1 cup apple cider vinegar
1/8 cup Worcestershire sauce
1-2 tablespoons hot sauce

• Combine ingredients in sauce pan and simmer, stirring. Serve hot.

• Makes about 4 3/4 cups.

Basil Dip

Serve this low calorie drip with crackers, fresh vegetables or chips.

1 cup plain yogurt
1/2 cup fresh basil leaves, chopped
1/2 medium cucumber, shredded, drained
2 teaspoons olive oil
2 sprigs fresh thyme leaves, stems removed (or 1/4 teaspoon dried)
1/2 teaspoon fresh lemon juice
Dash salt and pepper

• Combine ingredients, mixing well. Chill for an hour before serving.

• Makes about 1 1/2 cups.

Basil & Cheese Dip

Fresh basil is a summertime treat. It goes well with a variety of foods including raw vegetable sticks and crackers.

1 8-ounce package cream cheese, softened
1 cup grated Parmesan cheese
1 cup finely chopped walnuts
1/8 cup chopped fresh basil
1/8 cup olive oil
1 clove garlic, minced, or 1/8 teaspoon garlic powder
1/2 teaspoon fresh lemon juice

• Mix together ingredients in bowl until well blended. Refrigerate at least an hour for the flavors to combine, then serve at room temperature.

• Makes about 3 cups.

Basil & Green Onion Dip

Fresh basil gives this it's fresh, summery flavor. Serve it with just about anything from chips to crackers to fresh vegetables. Outstanding with jicama sticks or cucumber slices!

1 8-ounce package cream cheese, softened
1 cup sour cream
1/4 cup finely shredded carrot
1/3 cup chopped fresh basil
4 green onions, diced
Dash black pepper and salt
1/2 teaspoon fresh lemon juice
3 or 4 drops hot sauce

• Beat the cream cheese and sour cream together, then mix in the remaining ingredients and refrigerate to let flavors blend. Serve at room temperature.

• Makes about 2 cups.

Basil Pesto Dip

Yogurt and fresh pesto make this a tasty but light dip. Serve it on crackers or small rounds of toast.

1 cup plain yogurt
2 cups fresh loose-packed basil leaves
2 cloves garlic
1/2 cup pine nuts or lightly toasted pecans
2 tablespoons light vegetable oil

• Combine ingredients in food processor and pulse-process until almost smooth.

• Makes about 1 3/4 cups.

Beach Party Shrimp Dip

It's not necessary to have a beach in order to serve this dip. It's good anywhere and goes well with boiled, peeled shrimp.

1 cup mayonnaise
2 green onions, diced
1/4 cup finely chopped fresh parsley, (1 tablespoon reserved)
1 clove garlic, minced fine
Juice of 1/2 lemon
1/2 teaspoon hot sauce
1 teaspoon capers, minced
1 teaspoon anchovies, minced, or 1/4 teaspoon anchovy paste
1 tablespoon dill pickle, chopped fine
1 tablespoon Dijon mustard
2 teaspoons, or more, horseradish

• Mix ingredients together, mounding up in dip serving bowl. Top with 1 tablespoon chopped fresh parsley and surround with plenty of boiled shrimp.

• Makes about 1 1/2 cups.

Beefy Football Bean Dip

Serve this hearty dip to the t.v. football game crowd, or to a pack of hungry teenagers.

1 pound lean ground beef
1/2 cup chopped onion
1 teaspoon chili powder
1/2 cup catsup
1/4 teaspoon cayenne pepper
Dash of salt
1 4-ounce can chopped mild green chilies, drained
1 16-ounce can undrained red kidney beans
1 cup shredded sharp cheddar or American cheese
1 green spring onion, diced

• Cook ground beef with 1/2 cup chopped onion and chili powder until meat is browned and onion is tender. Stir in catsup and salt. Add chopped chilies and beans; mash mixture well. Heat in oven, then top with cheese and remaining diced spring onion. Keep beef and bean dip warm and serve with tortilla chips.

• Makes about 4 cups.

Catsup is listed in several dip recipes throughout the book. Did you know that catsup (also spelled ketchup), as we know it today is an American invention, but not totally? The first published recipe is from 1812, recorded by James Mease, a prominent Philadelphia doctor and horticulturist. But tomatoes, which are indigenous to the Americas, weren't always the primary ingredient in catsup. Originally the condiment was a salty anchovy sauce; the name comes from Indonesia, where the salty fish and soy sauce was called kecap ikan, and kecap was pronounced ketchup. The English, who traded with Indonesia for spices, adopted the sauce, as well as the word ketchup, and it remained a fishy sauce until the English landed in the Americas. Tomatoes and spices, with sugar and vinegar, make up our modern day catsup, but it's origins date back centuries to that early salted fish sauce.

Bell Pepper Dip

A creamy pepper dip with the flavor of roasted peppers, with less work (frying the peppers gives them a taste similar to roasting).

1 green bell pepper
1 red bell pepper
1 yellow bell pepper
1 shallot, cut up,
  or 2 tablespoons diced onion
2 tablespoons oil
1 cup sour cream
3/4 cup mayonnaise
1 tablespoons grated Parmesan cheese
1 teaspoon paprika
1 tablespoon fresh parsley, chopped

• Remove seeds and stems from peppers and cut up into food processor with the shallot or onion. Pulse blend until well chopped. Scrape the peppers and shallot into a skillet with the oil and fry on medium heat, about 10 minutes, stirring often until the peppers darken a bit in color. Remove from heat, drain off any liquid and let cool. Add remaining ingredients to pepper/shallot mixture in food processor and process until smooth. Refrigerate for at least an hour for flavors to blend.

• Makes about 2 1/2 cups.

Bell Pepper & Cheese Dip

Use this as a dip, or a sandwich spread for little bite-sized sandwiches. I use a mixture of cheeses for this, combining sharp cheddar, American, some Velveta and gouda or farmer's cheese. Use what you have on hand.

16 ounces any kind cheese, cut in cubes
1 3 1/2-ounce package cream cheese, softened
1 sweet red or yellow bell pepper, seeded, cut in pieces
4 tablespoons Miracle Whip
Small dash ground celery seed

• Combine cheese cubes and cream cheese in a food processor and pulse blend. Add the remaining ingredients and pulse blend until well chopped but lots of bits of pepper remain. Don't over-process. Refrigerate until ready to serve, then return to room temperature.

• Makes about 1 3/4 cups.

Billy Goat's Cucumber Onion Dip

We raise milk goats and as you know, they'll eat most anything, including cucumbers and onions and probably even this dip if you'd share it with them. Use as a dip for crisp vegetables or hot barbecue chips; it's delicious with barbecued hot wings, too.

1 cucumber, peeled, grated and drained, about 1/2 cup
1 8-ounce package cream cheese, softened
1 spring onion, diced
1/2 cup plain yogurt
2 tablespoons mayonnaise
1 tablespoon buttermilk
1/8 teaspoon hot sauce
Dash salt
Green food coloring, optional

• Combine ingredients in food processor and pulse blend.

• Makes about 1 3/4 cups.

Black Bean Hummus

In this version of hummus, black beans are used instead of the traditional cannelini beans, which gives it a darker, richer color and taste. Good served with toasted corn tortillas or corn chips. Jicama slices are also good with this.

1 16-ounce can black beans, drained
1 tablespoon tahini (sesame paste)
3 tablespoons extra virgin olive oil
Juice of 1 fresh lime
2 cloves garlic
1/2 teaspoon ground cumin
1 tablespoon freshly chopped parsley
Dash salt and pepper

• Combine ingredients in food processor and blend until smooth. Refrigerate until ready to use, then serve at room temperature.

• Makes about 1 1/2 cups.

Blue Cheese Dip

This is a delicious dip served with chilled, tart apples or crispy pear slices.

1 8-ounce package cream cheese, softened
3 tablespoons buttermilk
3 tablespoons mayonnaise
1/2 teaspoon Worcestershire sauce
1/2 cup crumbled blue cheese

• Blend cream cheese, milk, mayonnaise and Worcestershire sauce. Fold in blue cheese.

• Makes about 1 1/2 cups.

Blue Cheese & Cranberry Dip

1 3 1/2-ounce package cream cheese, softened
1/2 cup blue cheese salad dressing
1/4 cup blue cheese crumbles
1/4 cup whole-berry cranberry sauce
3/4 tablespoon Worcestershire sauce
1 tablespoon diced green onion or chives
1 teaspoon fresh lemon juice
Dash hot sauce

• Mix together cream cheese and salad dressing until smooth, then stir in remaining ingredients. Chill, then serve with crackers.

• Makes 1 1/2 cups.

Blue Cheese Dip, Quick

1 cup sour cream
1/3 cup buttermilk
4 ounces blue cheese crumbles
1/2 teaspoon hot sauce
1/2 teaspoon Worcestershire sauce

• Mix all ingredients; cover and refrigerate dip until ready to serve.

• Makes about 1 1/2 cups.

Caesar Dip

Created with the taste of Caesar dressing, this dip goes well with fresh vegetables or toast wedges. Try it with sweet bell pepper sections, too.

3 cups plain yogurt
1/4 cup grated Parmesan cheese
1 tablespoon Dijon mustard
1 tablespoon olive oil
1 clove garlic
1/4 teaspoon anchovy paste
Dash salt and freshly ground black pepper
Dash Worcestershire sauce

- Combine all ingredients in food processor and pulse blend.
- Makes 3 1/4 cups.

Caesar Dip, English Version

A bit richer version than the one above, this goes well with fish, fresh vegetables, chips or crackers.

1 1/2 cups sour cream
1/2 cup Romano cheese, finely grated
1 tablespoon freshly chopped parsley
1/4 teaspoon onion powder
1/4 teaspoon garlic powder
1/4 teaspoon dry mustard
1 teaspoon anchovy paste
Hefty dash freshly ground black pepper
2 teaspoons fresh lemon juice

- Combine ingredients in bowl and mix.
- Makes about 2 cups.

Cajun Caviar Dip

A non-cheesy, relatively healthy dip that guests like. If you are making several dips for a party, be sure to include this for a light contrast to some of the heavier dips. Serve with crackers or scoop-type chips.

2 16-ounce cans blackeyed peas, drained
1 jalapeno pepper, seeded, minced
2 green onions, diced fine
1/4 cup red or green bell pepper, diced
1/3 cup Italian salad dressing
2 teaspoons ground cumin
1 teaspoon Cajun spice
1/4 teaspoon cayenne pepper
Juice of 1/2 lemon
1/4 teaspoon sugar

• Combine ingredients, mixing well. Refrigerate for a few hours before serving for flavors to blend.

• Makes about 2 1/2 cups.

Cheesy Chipotle Dip

Corn chips, tortilla chips or fresh vegetable sticks all go well with this dip.

2 1/2 cups Velveeta cheese cubes
1 7-ounce can chipotle peppers in adobo sauce, chopped with juice
1 1/2 cups sour cream
3 green onions, diced fine
1 sprig marjoram, stem removed or 1/8 teaspoon dried

• Combine the Velveeta, chipotle peppers with their juice in a microwaveable bowl and microwave for about 3 minutes or until cheese is melted, stirring after about 2 minutes. Stir in the sour cream and chopped green onions and serve while warm.

• Makes about 4 1/3 cups.

Cheddar Beer Fondue

Serve this in a heated fondue pot with toasted bread cubes and fondue forks. Use a medium to dark beer for heartier flavor.

4 cups shredded sharp cheddar cheese
1 tablespoon flour
1 1/2 teaspoons dry mustard
1/8 teaspoon cayenne pepper
3/4 cup beer
2 teaspoons Worcestershire sauce

• Combine cheese, flour, mustard and cayenne in a bowl and mix. In the fondue pot, combine beer and Worcestershire sauce. Set temperature at 375° and heat until bubbling. Gradually add cheese mixture and stir constantly until cheese melts and mixture is smooth, about 5 minutes. Reduce temperature to keep it warm but not bubbling and serve.

• Makes about 4 cups.

Cheddar Dip

Serve this delicious cheesy dip with crackers or anything toasted.

2 cups shredded extra sharp cheddar cheese
1/3 cup Miracle Whip
2 tablespoons sour cream
2 green onions, diced
2 tablespoons red bell pepper, diced
1/2 teaspoon Worcestershire sauce
1/2 teaspoon hot sauce
3 or 4 leaves fresh or dried basil

• Combine cheese and Miracle Whip in food processor and process until fairly smooth. Add remaining ingredients and pulse blend to mix.

• Makes 2 1/2 cups.

Cheddar Jalapeno Cheese Dip

Delicious with crackers or spread on sweet bell pepper wedges or cucumber slices.

1/4 cup mayonaise
1 cup shredded sharp cheddar cheese
2 tablespoons fresh parsley, chopped fine
1 whole, fresh jalapeno pepper, seeds removed, chopped fine
1/4 teaspoon cayenne pepper, optional
2 teaspoons Worcestershire sauce

• Combine ingredients, mixing well. Chill for an hour or more for flavors to combine. Serve at room temperature.

• Makes about 1 1/4 cups.

Chili Cheese Dip

Serve this in a crockpot or chafing dish so it stays hot, with corn chips.

2 pounds lean ground beef
2 medium onions, chopped
3 jalapeno peppers, diced, seeds removed
3 tablespoons chili powder
1 can condensed tomato soup
1 16-ounce can tomato sauce
Salt and pepper to taste
1 pound Velveeta cheese, cubed

• Brown the beef with the onion, jalapenos and chili powder. Drain off any liquid. Add tomato soup and tomato sauce, then add Velveeta. Simmer on low heat, stirring, until cheese is melted. Top with shredded cheddar cheese and diced green onions.

• Makes 4-5 cups.

Chiles Con Queso Dip

Serve this with corn chips or green pepper wedges.

1/4 cup butter or margarine
1/2 cup chopped onion
1 seranno pepper, seeded and diced
1 can (about 15 ounces) diced tomatoes with liquid
2 4-ounce cans chopped mild green chiles, drained
16 ounces Monterey Jack cheese, cubed
1/2 cup heavy cream
1 spring onion, diced or 2 teaspoons diced chives

• In a large nonstick skillet over medium low heat, melt butter and sauté onion and seranno pepper until tender. Add tomatoes and chiles, mashing tomatoes with a spoon or potato masher. Simmer, stirring, about 15 minutes. Add cheese cubes, stirring until cheese is melted. Add cream and continue to cook, stirring constantly, for a couple of minutes longer. Remove from heat and let stand for 5 minutes. Serve in chafing dish or mini slow cooker and top with chopped spring onion.

• Makes about 5 cups.

Chive Dip

Make this with fresh chives. If you don't have fresh ones, use fresh green onion tops.

1 cup Miracle Whip
1 cup plain nonfat yogurt
2 tablespoons chopped fresh chives
1/8 teaspoon cayenne pepper or 1/4 teaspoon hot sauce
1/2 teaspoon onion powder
1/4 teaspoon Worcestershire sauce

• Combine ingredients and mix, then refrigerate for an hour or more before serving.

• Makes about 2 cups.

Clam Dip, Beach Club

Serve this with toasted pita bread.

1 3 1/2-ounce package cream cheese, softened
1 6 1/2-ounce can minced clams, drained, juice reserved
1/4 teaspoon black pepper
1/2 teaspoon cooking sherry
1 tablespoon parsley, chopped fine
1 green spring onion, diced fine
2 tablespoons sour cream
1 teaspoon fresh lemon juice
2 cloves garlic, minced fine
1/8 teaspoon Worcestershire sauce

• Combine ingredients except for the reserved clam juice and mix well. If too thick, add some of the reserved clam juice until it's the right consistency for dipping. Discard remaining clam juice. Refrigerate until serving time.

• Makes about 1 1/4 cups.

What is pita bread?

Pita is a round, wheat flatbread made with yeast. It's a traditional bread found in Middle Eastern and Mediterranean cuisines from North Africa to the Arabian countries and into India. Lebanese, Syrian and Arabian cultures all use this flat, pocket bread.

Clam Dip, Rhode Island Style

This is an outstanding dip to serve with crackers and afternoon drinks. Make plenty, this will go fast.

1 6 1/4-ounce can minced clams, undrained
1 8-ounce package cream cheese, softened
2 teaspoons freshly squeezed lemon juice
1 1/2 teaspoons Worcestershire sauce
1/4 teaspoon garlic salt
1/8 teaspoon freshly ground black pepper
1/4 teaspoon hot sauce

• Drain clams, measuring and saving 1/4 cup liquid. Mix clams, reserved liquid and remaining ingredients until well blended. Refrigerate an hour or more until chilled.

• Makes about 1 1/2 cups.

Cocktail Time Crab Dip

I like this best with hearty crackers or toast pieces, but it's also excellent with potato chips or raw vegetables.

3/4 cup catsup
2 tablespoons horseradish
1 8-ounce package cream cheese, softened
6 ounces (about 1/2 cup) crab meat, drained, flaked
1 green onion, diced, or 2 tablespoons fresh chives
2 tablespoons mayonnaise
1/8 teaspoon hot sauce
Few drops Worcestershire sauce

• Combine ingredients, mixing well. Refrigerate until serving time, then serve at room temperature.

• Makes about 2 cups.

Crab Dip

Crab dip is one of the most popular dips and there are lots of versions. This one's easy, quick and very good.

1 6-ounce can crab meat, drained and flaked
1 hard boiled egg, chopped
1/2 cup mayonnaise
2 tablespoons finely chopped fresh chives
2 teaspoons fresh lemon juice
1/2 teaspoon dry mustard
1/2 teaspoon onion powder
Dash salt and pepper

• Combine ingredients and mix, then cover and chill before serving.

• Makes about 1 1/4 cups.

Crab Dip, Baked

Serve this while hot with your favorite crackers or toasted bread pieces.

1 8-ounce package cream cheese, softened
1 6-ounce can crab meat, drained, flaked
2 tablespoons onion, grated
1 tablespoon half and half or milk
1/4 teaspoon Worcestershire sauce
Dash salt and black pepper
Few drops hot sauce
1 green onion, sliced

• Combine everything except green onion and mix together. Place in an ovenproof serving dish and bake at 350° F. for 15-18 minutes. Remove from oven and top with sliced green onion and serve.

• Makes about 1 3/4 cups.

Crab Dip, Baked, Cajun

1 8-ounce package cream cheese, softened
1 6-ounce can crab meat, drained, flaked
2 spring onions, diced
1 tablespoon horseradish
1 tablespoon half and half or milk
1 tablespoon mayonnaise
1/4 teaspoon hot sauce

- Combine and mix ingredients, then bake in an ovenproof serving dish for 15 minutes at 375° F.
- Makes about 2 cups.

Crab Dip, Island Style

A simple, quick to make dip that's good with crackers. It can be made the day before and returned to room temperature just before guests arrive.

1 8-ounce package cream cheese, softened
2 tablespoons Thousand Island dressing
2 tablespoons milk
1 6-ounce can crab meat, drained, flaked
2 tablespoons sweet red bell pepper, diced
Juice of 1 freshly squeezed lemon
1 tablespoon fresh parsley, chopped
Dash hot pepper sauce

- In a food processor combine cream cheese, dressing and milk, and mix well. Add remaining ingredients and pulse blend lightly. Refrigerate for at least an hour before serving.
- Makes about 1 1/2 cups.

Crab Shack Hot Crab Dip

You'll find this dip served at roadside crab shacks along the Gulf Coast. Best served hot with crackers, toast wedges or toasted pita pieces. Can be made ahead, and refrigerated or frozen, unbaked until right before guests arrive then bake.

1 3 1/2-ounce package cream cheese, softened
2 tablespoons mayonnaise
1/3 cup sour cream
1 tablespoon butter, softened
1/4 teaspoon Old Bay Seasoning, or seasoned salt
1/4 teaspoon paprika
1 green onion, diced fine
1 tablespoon red bell pepper, diced fine
1/3 cup Mozzarella cheese, grated
1 6-ounce can crab meat, drained, flaked
1/8 cup bread crumbs

- Preheat oven to 350° F. Mix together everything except bread crumbs and bake for 12 minutes, or until bubbly. Top with bread crumbs evenly and bake another 3 minutes. Serve hot.
- Makes about 1 1/2 cups.

Hot sauce.

Throughout the book you may find references to hot sauce. Sometimes known as pepper sauce, or Tobasco, there are hundreds, possibly thousands of brands, each different in flavor and degree of heat. Choose your favorite for any recipe calling for hot sauce.

Crab Dip, Faux

Here's a great crab dip recipe that uses imitation crab and is good with crackers, garlic toasts or raw vegetables.

2 spring onions, diced
1 stalk celery, cut in pieces
1 8-ounce package cream cheese, softened
8-10 ounces imitation crab, well chopped
1/2 cup sour cream
1/2 cup mayonnaise
1 tablespoon freshly chopped dill weed
Juice of 1/2 lemon

• In food processor, dice the onions and celery, then mix that together with the remaining ingredients. Refrigerate until ready to serve.

• Makes about 3 cups.

Cranberry Pecan Dip

We think of cranberries as a winter berry, but you can make this any time of year, holidays, as well. Serve with your favorite crackers or cucumber slices.

1 8-ounce package cream cheese, softened
2 tablespoons frozen orange juice concentrate
1 tablespoon honey
1/4 cup dried cranberries, chopped fine in food processor
2 teaspoons grated orange peel
1 teaspoon grated lemon peel
1/8 teaspoon ground cinnamon
1/4 cup pecans, coarsely chopped

• Combine cream cheese, orange juice and honey and mix until smooth. Add remaining ingredients, mixing again. Refrigerate until serving time, then return to room temperature before serving.

• Makes 1 1/2 cups.

Creamy Spinach Dip

1 cup mayonnaise
1 cup sour cream
1 10-ounce package frozen chopped spinach, thawed
1/2 cup chopped fresh parsley
5 green onions, chopped
2 teaspoons freshly squeezed lemon juice
1 teaspoon Worcestershire sauce
Dash of freshly ground black pepper

- Press or squeeze the thawed spinach to remove juice. Mix with remaining ingredients and chill in refrigerator for several hours before serving.
- Makes about 3 1/2 cups.

What is Worcestershire sauce?

Worcestershire sauce (pronounced *Wus-ter-shear*) is a widely used fermented liquid condiment. The modern version is made with vinegar, molasses, corn syrup, water, chili peppers, soy sauce, pepper, tamarinds, anchovies, onions, shallots, cloves and garlic. Filipino cooking often uses it as a marinade, especially with pork. It is one of the primary flavors in Caesar salad and in Bloody Marys.

The origin of Worcestershire sauce is thought to be the fermented anchovy sauce called *garum* which was a staple of Greco-Roman cooking. "Worcester sauce" as it was later called, is one of the legacies of British contact with India.

The recipe, in its current form, came from Sir Charles, Chief Justice of India in the 1830s. Two chemists, Lea & Perins, in Worcestershire, England, were shown the recipe and reproduced it and soon after went into production and the first bottles of the famous sauce were put on sale to the public in 1838. Lea & Perins is still the biggest producer of Worcestershire sauce.

The Japanese tonkatsu, yakisoba, and okonomiyaki sauces are all similar to Worcestershire sauce, but differ in their levels of sweetness and tartness.

Creamy Spinach, Low Cal

Use this as a dip for vegetables or a spread for crackers.

2 cups plain yogurt, drained*
1 10-ounce package frozen chopped spinach, thawed
1/2 cup low-fat ricotta cheese
1/2 cup grated Parmesan cheese
1/2 cup minced spring onions
2 tablespoons chopped fresh dill, or 1 tablespoon dry
Salt and pepper, to taste
Dash hot sauce

*Pour yogurt into strainer or cloth and drain for 15-20 minutes to remove some of the liquid. Combine ingredients and mix, then refrigerate for half an hour before serving.

- Makes about 4 cups.

Cucumber Dip with Cream Cheese

Simple, easy and delicious dip for summertime parties.

1 8-ounce package cream cheese, softened
1/2 cup sour cream
2 green onions, diced
1 medium cucumber, peeled, seeded
2 tablespoons mayonnaise
Dash salt and freshly ground black pepper
1/8 teaspoon hot sauce
1/2 teaspoon lemon juice

- In food processor, combine green onion and cucumber, pulse processing until chopped fine. Drain, pressing to remove excess juice from cucumber. Add the remaining ingredients and pulse blend. Pour into a bowl, garnish with cucumber slices if desired and refrigerate until ready to serve.

- Makes about 1 3/4 cups.

Cucumber-Dill Ranch Dip

A tasty combination for dipping raw vegetables such as jicama, carrot, celery or tomato wedges. Good on crackers and chips, too.

1 cucumber, peeled and seeded
1 green onion, diced
2 tablespoons fresh dill weed or 1 tablespoon dry
1 8-ounce package cream cheese, softened
1/4 cup ranch dressing
1/2 cup sour cream
1/4 teaspoon hot sauce
1/2 teaspoon lemon juice
Dash salt and freshly ground black pepper

• Chop cucumber, onion and fresh dill in food processor, then drain, pressing well to remove juice; combine with remaining ingredients, mixing well. Refrigerate until ready to serve.

• Makes about 1 1/2 cups.

Cucumber Tofu Dip

If you are looking for a dip that doesn't include dairy products, the tofu gives this a creamy texture just as if it had sour cream as an ingredient. Serve it with pita bread toasts or chips.

1 large cucumber, peeled, seeded
2 green onions, diced
1 pound package firm tofu
Juice of one half lemon
2 garlic cloves
1/2 teaspoon ground coriander
1/2 teaspoon ground cumin
Dash cayenne pepper and salt

• In a food processor, chop the cucumber and onions. Drain and squeeze out excess juice then in a mixing bowl, combine the cucumber and onion with the remaining ingredients and mix. Taste; if too tart, add 1/4 teaspoon honey.

• Makes about 2 cups.

Curry Garlic Dip

Delicious served with cold, boiled shrimp, crackers, or lightly blanched asparagus or raw vegetables.

2 cups mayonnaise
3 tablespoons chili sauce
2 teaspoons curry powder
2 cloves garlic,
  or 2 teaspoons garlic powder
Dash salt and black pepper
1 tablespoon diced onion
1 tablespoon Worcestershire sauce

• Combine ingredients in food processor and blend until fairly smooth. Refrigerate until ready to serve.

• Makes about 2 1/8 cups.

Dill Dip

The fresh taste of dill gives this a wonderful summery flavor that blends well with chips, crackers or fresh vegetables.

1 cup sour cream
1 cup mayonnaise
3 cloves garlic, finely chopped
4 tablespoons finely
  chopped fresh dill
1 tablespoon freshly
  squeezed lemon juice
Dash hot pepper sauce
Dash freshly ground black
  pepper and salt

• Mix ingredients, then cover and chill in refrigerator for at least an hour before serving.

• Makes 2 1/4 cups.

Dill Dip #2

1 3 1/2-ounce package
cream cheese, softened
1 cup sour cream
5 pimento stuffed green olives, diced
1 green onion, diced
2 tablespoons fresh dillweed,
or 1 tablespoon dry
1 teaspoon lemon juice
2-3 drops hot sauce

• Combine ingredients, mixing well.

• Makes about 1 1/3 cups.

Five Layer Seafood Dip

1 8-ounce package cream
cheese, softened
2 teaspoons horseradish
1/2 teaspoon Worcestershire sauce
1 tablespoon mayonnaise
Juice of 1/2 lemon
1/2 cup chili sauce
6 spring onions, diced
2/3 cup cucumber, peeled, diced
2 cups shrimp, cooked,
peeled and diced
1/4 cup grated cheddar cheese
1/8 cup canned jalapeno
peppers, diced

• Combine cream cheese, horseradish, Worcestershire sauce, mayonnaise and lemon juice, mixing together. Spread in the bottom of a 6 x 9 inch dish. Over that, spread the chili sauce, and top that with the diced cucumbers and onions. Top that layer with diced shrimp. Top the shrimp with diced jalapeno peppers and the cheddar cheese. Refrigerate until ready to serve.

• Makes about 4 1/4 cups.

The French have lent their name to a lot of foods in America, not always willingly or knowingly. Probably if you travel to France and look for French onion dip in the store, you won't find it. There are lots of versions of this old favorite, and here are a few of my personal favorites.

French Onion Dip, Hot

Serve this with dry, toasted French bread pieces, crackers or chips.

1 envelope any brand onion soup mix
2 cups sour cream
1 cup shredded cheese, like Swiss or cheddar
1/4 cup mayonnaise
1/4 teaspoon hot sauce
1 green onion or chives, diced
Dash freshly ground black pepper
1/2 cup additional shredded cheese, like Swiss or cheddar

- Preheat oven to 375° F. Combine ingredients in oven proof serving dish and bake for 20 minutes. Sprinkle with remaining grated cheese and bake until melted and bubbly. Serve hot.
- Makes about 4 cups.

French Onion Dip, Traditional

What makes it French? The method of browning the onions first, otherwise it would be just onion dip. Always good with chips or fresh vegetables, great with carrot sticks and cucumber slices, too.

1/2 tablespoon butter
1 cup finely chopped sweet onion
2 tablespoons Worcestershire sauce
1 8-ounce container sour cream
1/2 cup mayonnaise
Dash salt and black pepper

- Melt butter in a skillet and add the onion. Cook until tender and lightly browned, about 3-5 minutes on medium heat. Remove from heat and cool, then stir in Worcestershire sauce and remaining ingredients. Cover and refrigerate an hour or more to allow flavors to blend.
- Makes about 2 cups.

French Onion Dip, Zippy

Serve with chips.

1 Vidalia or Wallawalla sweet onion, peeled, sliced
1/4 cup butter
1/2 cup mayonnaise
1/2 cup sour cream
1/4 teaspoon ground cayenne pepper
Dash salt

• Melt butter in a saucepan and add the sliced onion. Simmer onion on low heat, stirring occasionally, about 20 minutes or until onions are lightly browned and soft. Combine onions with remaining ingredients in food processor and pulse blend until smooth but leaving some flecks of onions.

• Makes about 1 1/2 cups.

Green Chili Salsa Dip

This is a pleasantly hot dip that goes well with corn chips or crackers. For a nice variation, add 1 cup sour cream to this recipe and it becomes a completely different dip for chips.

8-10 fresh tomatillos, stemmed, husked, quartered
1/2 cup onion, diced
5 fresh jalapeno peppers, seeded, quartered
4 tablespoons fresh cilantro, chopped
2 cloves garlic
Juice of 1 fresh lime
2 tablespoons olive oil
1 1/2 teaspoons fresh tarragon, chopped, or 2 teaspoons dry
1/2 teaspoon sugar
Dash salt and black pepper

• Combine ingredients in food processor and pulse blend until coarsely chopped, then refrigerate for an hour or more. Serve at room temperature, or chilled.

• Makes about 4 cups.

Green Goddess Dip

Much like the famous green goddess salad dressing (named in honor of a movie by that name), this is a delicious dip. It's the anchovies that give it the familiar green goddess flavor. Serve this with breadsticks, crackers, potato chips or most anything else dippable.

2 cups mayonnaise
1/2 cup sour cream
2 tablespoons tarragon vinegar, <u>or</u>
2 tablespoons white wine vinegar and 2 teaspoons dry tarragon
2 tablespoons fresh chives, chopped, or 1 green onion top
2 teaspoons anchovy paste
Dash salt and pepper
3-4 drops hot sauce

• Combine ingredients in food processor and pulse blend. Refrigerate for a few hours to let flavors blend, or make a day ahead of party time.

• Makes about 2 3/4 cups.

Green Onion Dip, #1

When guests arrive without much notice, you can toss this together in just minutes.

4 green onions, chopped
1 1/2 cups sour cream
1/2 cup mayonnaise
1/4 teaspoon garlic powder, or 1 clove garlic, minced
1/8 teaspoon hot sauce
2-3 drops Worcestershire sauce

• Combine ingredients, mixing well. Refrigerate for at least 2 hours for flavors to blend before serving, or serve immediately if you're in a hurry.

• Makes about 2 1/8 cups.

Green Onion Dip #2

2 cups cottage cheese
8 green onions, cut in pieces
1/4 cup mayonnaise
Dash cayenne pepper
1/8 teaspoon Worcestershire sauce
2 teaspoons diced chives for garnish

• Put ingredients in food processor and blend until fairly smooth. Refrigerate until serving time.

• Makes 2 1/2 cups.

Green Onion & Cheese Dip

Simple and tasty, you can also make this low-calorie by using low-fat, low calorie ingredients.

2 cups cottage cheese
2 tablespoons mayonnaise
6 coarsely chopped green onions
1/4 cup fresh parsley
Dash salt
1/2 teaspoon hot sauce
1 tablespoon fresh lemon juice.

• Combine ingredients in a food processor and pulse blend. Cover and refrigerate for at least an hour.

• Makes about 2 1/2 cups.

Green Pea Dip

A bright green, very tasty dip for any kind of dippers.

1 avocado, peeled, seeded, diced
Juice of 1 fresh lime
1 16-ounce package frozen green peas
1/2 cup plain yogurt
1 green onion, diced
1 clove garlic, minced
1 tablespoon chopped fresh cilantro
1 Roma tomato, seeded, diced
Tiny dash ground cumin
Dash salt

• Squeeze lime over diced avocado and set aside. Place peas in strainer and run hot tap water over them until thawed and bright green. Combine peas and yogurt in food processor and process until smooth. Transfer to bowl and mix in remaining ingredients, then refrigerate until ready to serve.

• Makes about 2 3/4 cups.

Green Pea & Avocado Dip

This dip is a lot like guacamole and it's simple and easy, plus healthier and lower in calories than regular avocado dip.

1 small avocado, peeled, seeded, diced
Juice of 1/2 lemon
1 10-ounce package frozen peas, thawed
4 green onions, diced
1/2 cup loosely packed cilantro leaves
1 anaheim or jalapeno pepper, seeded, quartered
5 Roma tomatoes, diced

• Combine avocado and half of the lemon juice in a bowl and set aside.

• In food processor, blend peas until smooth, then add the onions, remaining lemon juice, cilantro and pepper and pulse blend. Pour out contents of the food processor into a bowl. Add avocado and tomatoes and gently mix. Refrigerate for 30 minutes to let flavors combine.

• Makes about 2 1/4 cups.

Green Pea Guacamole

It's like guacamole, but without the avocados. Why make it? Because it's easy and tastes really good, and is lower in calories. Any favorite chips go well with this.

2 10-ounce packages frozen peas, thawed, drained
4 green onions, chopped
2 cloves garlic
2 teaspoons fresh lemon juice
1/4 cup fresh cilantro, chopped
1/2 teaspoon hot sauce
Dash salt and pepper

• Combine peas, onion and garlic in food processor and process until smooth. Stir in remaining ingredients, mixing, then refrigerate for at least an hour for flavors to blend.

• Makes about 2 cups.

Guacamole

Fresh and delicious, serve this with your favorite corn chips.

3 avocados, peeled, seeded
Juice of 1 fresh lime
2 green onions, diced
2 cloves garlic, minced fine
1 ripe tomato, seeded, diced
1/4 cup freshly chopped cilantro
Salt to taste

• Mash avocados with lime juice, then add remaining ingredients. If making more than a few hours before serving, cover bowl with plastic wrap and force out the air to prevent browning.

• Makes about 1 1/2 cups.

Guacamole & Shrimp Dip

Chips, crackers, toasted pita bread, bread sticks, cucumber slices or jicama slices, all go well with this dip.

3 avocados, peeled, seeded
2 cloves garlic, minced
1 1/2 cups small cooked shrimp, chopped
1 tablespoon olive oil
1 green onion, diced
1 cup sour cream
1/4 cup green pimento stuffed olives, diced
1/2 cup parsley, chopped
1 tablespoon chili sauce or catsup
1/2 teaspoon Worcestershire sauce

• Mash avocados and add remaining ingredients, mixing well. Refrigerate for at least an hour before serving.

• Makes about 3 1/2 cups.

Hawaiian Dip

Serve this with celery or jicama sticks, crispy crackers or grilled chicken wings. The addition of the lemon verbena or basil makes this an outstanding and out-of-the-ordinary dip.

1 3 1/2-ounce package cream cheese, softened
1/2 cup sour cream
1 8-ounce can crushed pineapple, drained
1/4 cup *mango chutney
2 teaspoons fresh lemon verbena or lemon basil, chopped fine
1/8 teaspoon cayenne

• Combine ingredients in bowl and beat together with a spoon until well mixed. Refrigerate until ready to serve.

• Makes about 2 cups.

* Or substitute peach preserves.

Herb Curry Dip

Serve with fresh vegetables like jicama, carrots and celery. This is also good with boiled egg slices on crackers.

1 cup mayonnaise
1/2 cup sour cream
1 tablespoon fresh parsley, chopped
2 4-inch sprigs fresh thyme, stem discarded,
or 1 teaspoon dry, crushed
1 green onion, chopped fine
2 teaspoons fresh lemon juice
1/2 teaspoon Worcestershire sauce
1/2 teaspoon curry powder
1 teaspoon capers, minced

- Mix ingredients and refrigerate until ready for serving. Taste and adjust amount of curry seasoning; add more to taste.
- Makes about 1 1/2 cups.

Hollandaise Sauce Dip

Make this to use as a dipping sauce for barely cooked, still crisp, fresh asparagus. This dip also works well with barely steamed broccoli, as well as with avocado slices on crackers.

4 egg yolks
6 tablespoons fresh lemon juice
1 cup butter
1/2 cup mayonnaise
1 teaspoon dry tarragon

- In small saucepan, stir egg yolks and lemon juice until they are well mixed. Cut up the butter and add to the lemon-egg mixture and simmer, stirring, over very low heat until butter is melted and sauce thickens. Cook slowly, continuing to stir, then remove mixture from heat as soon as sauce thickens. Stir briefly to cool, then add the 1/2 cup mayonnaise and tarragon. Mix and refrigerate until ready to serve.
- Makes about 1 1/2 cups.

Crisp steamed asparagus.

Cut tough bottom ends from fresh asparagus. Bring 4 cups of water to a boil in a pan and drop in the asparagus spears (or use an asparagus steamer basket). Simmer for 30-45 seconds. Remove and rinse quickly in iced water to stop the cooking process and refrigerate the spears until ready to use. Arrange around a bowl of Hollandaise Sauce for dipping.

Hollandaise Dipping Sauce, Blender Style

3 egg yolks
2 tablespoons fresh lemon juice
1/4 teaspoon salt
Dash cayenne pepper
1/2 cup butter

• Put egg yolks, lemon juice, salt and cayenne pepper in blender and pulse blend, and set aside. Melt butter in microwave. With blender on low speed, slowly pour butter in a steady stream. The mixture will emulsify, or thicken, and is ready to use while still warm.

• Makes about 3/4 cup.

Honey-Lime Dip for Fruit

A delicious dip for fruit; try this with fresh pineapple wedges, strawberries, melon pieces, grapes, fresh peaches or plums.

1 cup vanilla yogurt
2 tablespoons honey
2 tablespoons fresh lime juice
1 teaspoon lime zest
Light dash cayenne pepper

• Mix ingredients and refrigerate until ready to use.

• Makes about 1 1/8 cup.

Honey Mustard Dip

Serve this with pretzels or bread sticks, or use it to spread on crackers and top with tiny cold cuts.

1/2 cup mayonnaise
3 tablespoons Dijon mustard
3 tablespoons honey

- Combine and mix together.
- Makes about 2/3 cup.

Honey Yogurt Dip

Serve this with fresh fruit for dipping. Strawberries, grapes, cantaloupe, honeydew, kiwi slices, and other favorite seasonal fruits, work well.

1 8-ounce container vanilla yogurt
1 tablespoon honey
Dash cinnamon

- Combine, mixing well.
- Makes about 1 cup.

Horseradish Dip

Serve with chilled carrot sticks, celery, jicama, cucumber or turnip slices as well as hearty crackers. Also good with cooked, peeled shrimp, or grilled pork or ham on toothpicks.

3 tablespoons half and half or milk
2 cups cottage cheese
2 tablespoons, or more, horseradish
1/2 teaspoon Worcestershire sauce
1 tablespoon chopped fresh parsley
Dash salt
1/8 teaspoon hot sauce

- Put all ingredients in food processor and process until smooth.
- Makes 2 1/8 cups.

Hot Buffalo Chicken Dip

Serve with celery sticks or chips that have some substance and won't easily break, such as corn chips, pita chips, etc. Toasted pita triangles go well with this, too.

4 cooked chicken breasts, diced
3 tablespoons any favorite hot sauce
2 8-ounce packages cream cheese, softened
1 cup ranch dressing
1/2 cup celery, diced
2 green onions, chopped
2 tablespoons sweet bell pepper, diced
1 seranno or jalapeno pepper, seeded, diced
8 ounces grated sharp cheddar cheese

• In the bottom of a 13 x 9 x 2 inch baking pan, spread the diced chicken. Combine the hot sauce, softened cream cheese and ranch dressing, mix and pour that over the chicken. Spread celery, onion and peppers over that, then add the grated cheese. Bake for about 30 minutes or until bubbling. Serve warm.

• Makes approximately 4 cups.

Hot Jalapeno & Olive Dip

Serve this dip hot, fresh out of the oven with corn chips.

1 cup shredded sharp cheddar cheese
1 cup mayonnaise
1/4 cup chopped black olives
1 4-ounce can diced jalapeno peppers
1 clove garlic, diced, or 1/4 teaspoon garlic powder
1/8 teaspoon hot sauce
1 tomato, chopped
4 green onions, diced, divided

• Preheat oven to 350° F. Combine everything except chopped tomato and half of the green onions and bake in a baking pan for 20 minutes. Serve hot with the remaining onions and chopped tomato on top.

• Makes about 3 cups.

Hot Honey Mustard Dip

Serve this with mini egg rolls, fried shrimp or chicken. It's quite hot, and sweet, so a little goes a long way.

2 tablespoons dry mustard powder
2 tablespoons water
1/4 cup honey, or more

• Combine mustard powder and water and mix. Set aside for at least 15 minutes for the mustard to reach it's full heat. Then add the honey, mix and taste. If still too hot for your taste, add a bit more honey.

• Makes about 1/4 cup.

Hot and Creamy Mustard Dip

Good with egg rolls, fried shrimp, chicken fingers or ham wedges.

3 tablespoons Chinese hot prepared mustard
1 3/4 cups sour cream
1/3 cup mayonnaise
1/2 teaspoon dry onion flakes
2 green spring onions, chopped fine
1/2 teaspoon paprika
1/2 teaspoon prepared yellow mustard

• Combine ingredients, mixing well. Refrigerate for at least an hour before serving.

• Makes about 2 1/4 cups.

Hot Oyster and Mushroom Dip

A good winter party dip to serve with French bread toasts, crackers, Melba toast, etc.

1/3 cup butter
1 cup sweet Vidalia or similar onions, chopped
1/2 cup red bell pepper, chopped
3/4 cup finely diced celery
1 clove garlic, minced
2 dozen fresh or frozen oysters, drained, chopped
1/2 teaspoon hot sauce
1/2 teaspoon paprika
1 can golden mushroom soup
Dash salt and black pepper
1 green onion, chopped
1 tablespoon fresh parsley, minced

• In skillet, melt butter and add onions, pepper, celery and garlic and sauté until tender. Add oysters and simmer, about 5 minutes. Add hot sauce, paprika and condensed soup, mixing, then simmer on low heat until bubbly. Add salt and pepper, pour hot into serving dip dish and top with chopped green onion and parsley.

• Makes about 4 cups.

Horseradish Bacon Dip

Great with crackers or raw vegetables such as jicama, even with chips.

2 cups shredded sharp cheddar cheese
1 cup sour cream
1/4 cup cooked, crumbled bacon
1 tablespoon horseradish
2 tablespoons chopped fresh chives, or 1 tablespoon dry

• Combine cheese, sour cream, bacon and horseradish in food processor and pulse blend until smooth. Stir in chives. Refrigerate for an hour to let flavors combine.

• Makes 3 1/4 cups.

Low-Cal Carrot Onion Dip

Good as a dip with few calories or fat, or use it for topping on baked potatoes. It's good in lots of ways. Also excellent with tortilla chips, fresh vegetables like jicama, or carrot sticks.

1 1/2 cup light cottage cheese
1 tablespoon freshly squeezed lemon juice
1 tablespoon carrot, finely grated
1 tablespoon minced chives or green onion
2 tablespoons fresh parsley, diced, or 1 tablespoon dry
1/2 teaspoon sugar
Dash black pepper
1/8 teaspoon hot sauce

• In a food processor, combine ingredients and pulse blend until fairly smooth.

• Makes about 1 3/4 Cups

Mustard Dip

Delicious dip for lightly steamed but still firm asparagus spears, cheese pieces, ham, etc.

1/4 cup honey
3 teaspoons vegetable oil
2 tablespoons prepared mustard
1 1/2 cups mayonnaise,
1/2 teaspoon garlic powder, or 1 clove garlic

• Combine ingredients in food processor and blend until smooth. Refrigerate until ready to serve.

• Makes 1 3/4 cups.

Mustard with Mustard Dip

Serve this quick and easy dip with cucumber or raw turnip slices, fish bites, toasted pita bread or French bread. Grilled mini hot dogs on toothpicks go great with this, too.

1/3 cup buttermilk
1 cup sour cream
1/4 cup Dijon mustard
2 teaspoons ground mustard
1/4 teaspoon brown sugar
1 green onion, diced fine
2 tablespoons fresh parsley, minced fine

• Combine everything except onion and parsley, mixing well. Put in serving dip bowl and top with diced green onions and parsley.
• Makes 1 2/3 cups.

Mustard Ranch Dip

This is my own version of this popular dip. It's good with pork, chicken, ham, roast beef, pretzels or crackers.

1 cup sour cream
1 cup mayonnaise
1 cup prepared yellow mustard
1/3 cup sugar or honey
1/4 cup dried onion flakes
2 teaspoons garlic powder
2 tablespoons prepared horseradish
1 1-ounce package ranch dressing mix

• Combine ingredients, mixing well. Refrigerate for an hour or more before serving.

• Makes about 3 1/2 cups.

Pepper Dip, Easy

When you make this, choose ripe, sweet bell peppers, either red or yellow ones (or both). Then, once the dip is made, make a dip serving bowl out of the largest green, yellow or red bell pepper you can find. First, cut the stem end off near the top, as if you were making a jack-o'lantern, leaving a lid with the stem intact. Remove the seed core and any insides. Level, if necessary by shaving a small portion off the bottom (but don't cut through or your "bowl" will leak). Fill with Pepper Dip and put the top back on to refrigerate until serving time.

1 sweet red bell pepper, cut in pieces
1 sweet yellow bell pepper, cut in pieces
1 tablespoon fresh chives, diced, or 2 teaspoons dry
2 tablespoons fresh parsley, cut up
1 teaspoon Worcestershire sauce
Dash black pepper and salt
1 cup sour cream
1 3 1/2-ounce package cream cheese, softened
1/3 cup mayonnaise

- Place the peppers, parsley and chives in a food processor and pulse blend until chopped. Remove to a mixing bowl and add remaining ingredients, mixing well. Refrigerate for an hour or more before serving.
- Makes about 2 2/3 cups.

Pepper Dip, Skillet Style

This isn't an "instant" dip because it does take a few minutes preparation time. However, it's delicious and if you're making it for a party, you can make double the amount in the same length of time as one smaller batch. If you like the flavor of roasted peppers, you will like this. Serve with crackers, pepper wedges, celery sticks or any other favorite dipper.

1 red bell pepper, seeded, cut in pieces
1 yellow bell pepper, seeded, cut in pieces
2 seranno or jalapeno peppers, seeded
1 clove garlic
1 medium onion, cut in pieces
2 tablespoon light vegetable oil
1 cup sour cream
1 8-ounce package cream cheese, softened
2 teaspoons soy sauce

• Combine peppers, garlic and onion in a food processor and pulse-blend until coarsely chopped. Place the chopped ingredients in a small nonstick skillet with the vegetable oil and heat to medium hot, stirring. Continue cooking and stirring the mixture until it darkens and becomes fragrant - about 10 minutes. Drain off any juice then pour ingredients into mixing bowl and cool; add the remaining ingredients and mix well. Leave at room temperature for about an hour before serving, or can be refrigerated overnight then brought back to room temperature to serve.

• Makes about 3 cups.

Pesto Dip

This dip combines the fresh basil and garden flavor of pesto, in a creamy dip. Melba toast, toasted pita wedges, crackers or raw vegetables all go well with this.

1/4 cup olive oil
1 cup fresh basil leaves, packed
1/2 cup parsley leaves, packed
1/2 cup grated Parmesan cheese
1/3 cup English walnuts
2 cloves garlic
1 teaspoon grated lemon rind
1/4 teaspoon black pepper
1 cup sour cream
1 tablespoon mayonnaise
2 teaspoons lemon juice
Dash salt.

• Combine basil, parsley, cheese, and garlic and pulse blend until coarsely chopped. Add walnuts and remaining ingredients and process until fairly smooth but still a bit lumpy.

• Makes about 2 1/4 cups.

Pimento Cheese Dip

You could make sandwiches out of this but it's so good as a dip you will probably eat it with cucumber slices, jicama or crackers.

1 5-ounce jar chopped pimentos
1 1/2 cups grated sharp cheddar cheese
1 cup mayonnaise
1/2 cup coarsely chopped pecans
2 tablespoons red bell pepper, diced fine

• Mix together ingredients, adding pecans and bell pepper last. Mix then refrigerate until ready to serve.

• Makes about 3 cups.

Pizza Dip, Hot

Serve this with bread sticks, chips or toasted pita bread triangles.

1 8-ounce package cream cheese, softened
1 teaspoon dry Italian seasoning spice blend,
or 1/4 teaspoon marjoram,
1/4 teaspoon oregano
1/2 teaspoon basil
1/4 teaspoon garlic powder
2 cups shredded Mozzarella cheese
1 cup shredded cheddar cheese
1/2 cup pizza sauce
1 green bell pepper, finely chopped
1 red bell pepper, finely chopped
Dash hot pepper sauce

• Preheat oven to 350° F. Lightly oil a 9 x 9 inch baking dish, then spread cream cheese over the bottom. Sprinkle Italian seasoning and garlic powder over cream cheese. Add the cheeses on top, spreading evenly. Top that by spreading the pizza sauce and peppers on top and bake for 15-20 minutes or until bubbly. Serve hot.

• Makes about 5 cups.

Quick Vegetable Dip

If you don't have time to make a more complicated dip, this still has good flavor and takes little effort. Make it at least an hour before you serve it, for the flavors to combine.

1 package dehydrated instant vegetable soup mix
1 cup mayonnaise
1 cup sour cream
3 tablespoons chopped fresh parsley
1 green onion or chives, diced
1/8 teaspoon Worcestershire sauce

• Combine and mix ingredients and refrigerate until ready to serve.

• Makes 2 1/8 cups.

Red Pepper Dip

Combining the sweet flavors of roasted peppers in a creamy dip, this is good with crackers, chips, fresh vegetables.

1 7-1/2 ounce jar roasted red peppers, drained
1/2 cup mayonnaise
1 8-ounce package cream cheese, softened
1/2 teaspoon garlic powder, or 1 clove garlic, minced
Dash freshly ground black pepper
1/8 teaspoon hot sauce

• Put ingredients except peppers, in food processor and pulse process until smooth. Add peppers and coarsely chop, leaving pieces of the peppers in the dip. Refrigerate for a few hours to blend flavors, then serve at room temperature.

• Makes about 1 1/2 cups.

Salmon Mousse Dip

Easy, quick, and so good you'll want to make extra for replacing it when the bowl gets empty on the party table. Serve this with good quality crackers. I first tasted this at the fabulous Dairy Hollow House Restaurant in Eureka Springs and went home and started reconstructing the recipe. This is my version and a favorite when I plan a party.

1 cup sour cream
1 8-ounce package cream cheese, softened
6-8 ounces smoked salmon, flaked
2 tablespoons mayonnaise
2 teaspoons Worcestershire sauce
1 teaspoon hot sauce
2 teaspoons freshly chopped chives, or 1 teaspoon dry

• Combine ingredients in a food processor and pulse process until salmon is chopped but still leaving plenty of pieces in the dip. Refrigerate until ready to serve then let come to room temperature.

• Makes about 2 1/2 cups.

Shrimp Dip

Serve this with your favorite crackers and it will disappear quickly on the party table. Shrimp lovers really like this one!

2 cups cooked shrimp, chopped fine
Juice of 1 lemon
1 8-ounce package cream cheese, softened
2 teaspoons Worcestershire sauce
3/4 cup catsup
1 tablespoon horseradish
2 green onions, diced fine
1/2 teaspoon cayenne pepper
Dash salt to taste

• Combine ingredients and mix well. Refrigerate for 2 hours or more before serving.

• Makes about 3 3/4 cups.

Shrimp Cocktail Dip

The traditional red sauce for dipping boiled or fried shrimp.

1 1/2 cups catsup
1 tablespoon Worcestershire sauce
1 tablespoon horseradish
2 teaspoons hot sauce
Juice of 1 lemon

• Combine ingredients and mix well. Chill until ready to serve.

• Makes 1 2/3 cups.

Shrimp Dip, California Style

1 package dry onion soup mix
3/4 cup sour cream
1 cup plain yogurt
1/4 cup any brand chili sauce
1/2 cup cooked, chopped shrimp
1 tablespoon horseradish
1/2 cup canned crab meat, chopped
1 teaspoon hot sauce
1 teaspoon fresh lemon juice

• Combine ingredients, mixing well. Refrigerate for at least an hour before serving.

• Makes about 2 1/2 cups.

Shrimp Dip, Gulf Shore

Serve this with toasted pita chips or substantial (meaning strong) crackers.

2 pounds cooked, peeled shrimp, chopped
Juice of 1 lemon
2 8-ounce packages cream cheese, softened
1/3 cup sour cream
3/4 cup catsup
5 green onions, chopped fine, or
3 tablespoons grated onion
1 tablespoon horseradish
1 teaspoon Worcestershire sauce
1 teaspoon hot sauce

• Combine ingredients, mixing well. Refrigerate 2 hours, or longer, before serving.

• Makes 5-6 cups.

Shrimp Mousse

Serve this molded mousse with butter crackers. It can be made a couple of days ahead and refrigerated.

1 8-ounce package cream cheese, cubed
1 can condensed tomato soup
2 tablespoons unflavored gelatin
1 1/2 pounds shrimp, cooked, peeled, diced
1 cup mayonnaise
3/4 cup celery, finely chopped
4 green onions, finely chopped
1/2 cup bell pepper, finely chopped
1 teaspoon Worcestershire sauce
2 teaspoons fresh lemon juice

• Combine cream cheese and soup and heat in microwave only until the cheese is soft. Mix, then cool slightly. Stir in gelatin, mixing well, then add remaining ingredients and mix again. Pour into a well oiled 1 quart, or larger, decorative mold. Cover and refrigerate overnight. Unmold onto platter and serve.

• Makes about 4 cups.

Shrimpy Mustard Dip

If you want a dip with some substance, this is it. Serve it with celery sticks, good quality crackers, hefty chips or your favorite dipper.

1 8-ounce package cream cheese, softened
1/4 cup Dijon mustard
1/4 cup sour cream
1 green onion, diced fine
1/2 cup cooked shrimp, chopped
1/4 teaspoon hot sauce
1 teaspoon fresh lemon juice

• Combine ingredients, mixing well. Chill several hours before serving.

• Makes about 2 cups.

Simple Salmon Dip

1 14-ounce can salmon, drained
1 8-ounce package cream cheese, softened
1/8 cup mayonnaise
1 clove garlic, minced
2 teaspoons freshly squeezed lemon juice
2 teaspoons chives, diced
2 tablespoons fresh parsley, chopped
Dash black pepper
Dash any favorite hot sauce
Pinch of celery salt

- Combine ingredients in food processor and pulse blend until almost smooth. Refrigerate at least an hour for flavors to blend before serving.
- Makes about 2 1/4 cups.

Smoked Oyster Dip

Chips, crackers or bread sticks all go well with this delicious dip.

1 8-ounce package cream cheese, softened
2 tablespoons mayonnaise
2 teaspoons freshly squeezed lemon juice
1/4 teaspoon garlic powder
Dash hot sauce
1 9-ounce can smoked oysters, drained, chopped
1/3 cup chopped black olives, optional

- Combine cream cheese, mayonnaise, lemon juice, garlic and hot sauce in a small bowl. Mix until well blended, then mix in smoked oysters (and optional black olives). Refrigerate until serving time.
- Makes about 1 1/2 cups.

Smoked Salmon Dip

Serve this once and your friends will ask you to make it at the next party. It's easy and can be made a day or two in advance if you choose.

1 8-ounce package cream cheese, softened
3/4 cup sour cream
Juice of 1/2 lemon
1 green onion, diced
1 teaspoon horseradish
1 1/2 cups smoked salmon, minced
1/2 cup toasted, chopped pecans
2 tablespoons fresh parsley, chopped

• Combine ingredients, except for pecans and parsley, mixing well. Transfer to serving bowl and top with pecans and parsley, then refrigerate for at least an hour. Let dip come to room temperature before serving.

• Makes about 3 1/2 cups.

Spinach Paté

Serve Spinach Paté with toasted French bread pieces or crackers. This is quick to make and delicious. It's not, however, the prettiest thing on the party table, so I suggest "icing" it like a cake, with some softened cream cheese, mixed with a tablespoon of mayonnaise, then topping that with some chopped fresh chives and parsley.

2 12-ounce containers frozen spinach, thawed
1/3 cup chopped shallots or green onions
1 garlic clove, sliced
3 eggs, beaten
3/4 cup heavy whipping cream
1/2 cup bread crumbs
1 teaspoon salt
1/4 teaspoon cayenne pepper
Dash black pepper
Dash hot sauce
2 tablespoons diced parsley

• Preheat oven to 350° F.
Drain and squeeze the spinach until fairly dry. Combine with remaining ingredients in food processor and pulse blend until smooth. Pour mixture into a well oiled 8 x 5 inch loaf pan. Set pan into a second dish in which you have poured water about 1 inch deep. Bake for about 50 minutes, or until firm. Cool and refrigerate for several hours or overnight. Unmold paté onto serving dish and cover with softened cream cheese and finely diced parsley.

• Makes about 3 1/2 cups.

Tarragon Mayonnaise Dip

*This dip goes especially well with crispy steamed and chilled asparagus spears, as well as with bread sticks, lettuce ribs or cucumber slices. If you live in the warmer parts of the U.S., Zone 7 or south, tarragon is harder to grow. You can substitute the same amount of Texas tarragon, also known as Mexican mint-marigold (*Tagetes lucida*) for the French tarragon. Texas tarragon is easier to grow, has a robust, pleasant tarragon flavor and lends itself to all sorts of culinary uses.*

2 cups mayonnaise
1/2 cup sour cream
2 tablespoons fresh tarragon, chopped
1 tablespoon white wine vinegar
1 green onion, chopped
1 tablespoon fresh parsley, chopped

- Combine ingredients in food processor and pulse blend briefly. Refrigerate for at least an hour or more before serving.
- Makes about 2 3/4 cups.

Texas Tarragon Mustard Dip

Grilled chicken strips, cooked shrimp or crispy steamed asparagus spears all are good with this dip.

1 tablespoon fresh Texas tarragon, chopped, or 2 teaspoons dry tarragon
1 tablespoon white wine vinegar
1 tablespoon Dijon mustard
Dash salt and black pepper
1 cup mayonnaise
1/2 cup sour cream

• Combine the tarragon, vinegar, salt and pepper, blending well. Mix in the mayonnaise, then the sour cream. Chill before serving.

• Makes about 1 1/2 cups.

What's Texas tarragon?

Also known as Mexican mint marigold, it's an herb that's easier to grow in the South than French tarragon, yet has a similar flavor. Botanical name, *Tagetes lucida*; use it as you would French tarragon, fresh or dry.

Tex-a-Looney Dip

Layered dips are popular because they're easy and look interesting on the party table. This comes from a Texas party-giver and I've changed it considerably for my own tastes. Originally it called for frozen avocados which makes as much sense as using frozen tomatoes. Use the freshest ingredients you can! It's a looney dip but darned good.

1/4 cup shredded cheese
2 16-ounce cans refried black beans
1 tablespoon hot sauce
1 8-ounce package cream cheese, softened
3 tablespoons fresh cilantro, finely chopped
1 10-ounce can diced tomatoes and chilies, drained
1/2 teaspoon garlic powder
3 fresh avocados, peeled, seeded, diced, tossed with:
Juice of 1 fresh lime
1 1/2 tablespoons taco seasoning
1 4-ounce can chopped green chilies
1 cup sour cream
6 green onions, diced
1 red bell pepper, diced
1 jalapeno pepper, diced
1/4 cup shredded sharp cheddar cheese
1/4 cup fresh parsley, chopped, mixed with:
1/4 cup fresh cilantro, chopped
2 cups grated cheddar cheese
2 ripe tomatoes, seeded, diced, drained

• In a serving pan, about 10 x 14 inches, spread the 1/4 cup shredded cheese. Then mix together the next 6 ingredients and spread evenly on top of the shredded cheese. Layer the remaining ingredients in the order they are listed, ending with the grated cheese, topped by the cilantro and parsley, mixed with tomatoes scattered on top. Press down just a bit to firm up the dip and refrigerate for at least an hour before serving. Can be made a day ahead of the party.

• Serves 12-15 people.

Tex-Mex Beany Avocado Dip

Simple ingredients makes this quick to put together. Serve with corn chips and some extra salsa, too.

1 16-ounce can refried black beans
2 avocados, peeled, seeded, diced
1 tablespoon canned green chilies
1 clove garlic
  or 1/2 teaspoon garlic powder
1 teaspoon any brand taco seasoning
1/2 cup sour cream
1 ripe tomato, diced and drained
1 green onion, diced
1 tablespoon diced fresh cilantro

• Place the refried beans, avocados, chilies, garlic, taco seasoning and sour cream in a food processor and pulse blend, leaving the mixture still a bit chunky. Mix in the diced tomato, then place mixture in a serving bowl and top with diced green onion and cilantro.

• Makes about 2 1/2 cups.

Three Cheese Dip

Serve this with crackers, toasted chapatti pieces, pita wedges, toasted nan bread cut in pieces or celery sticks.

1/2 cup mayonnaise
1/4 cup sour cream
1/4 cup white wine vinegar
1/2 cup grated Parmesan cheese
1/4 cup cottage cheese
1/4 cup blue cheese crumbles
1 clove garlic
1 teaspoon dry mustard
1 teaspoon Worcestershire sauce
2 teaspoons fresh chives, chopped

• Place ingredients in a food processor and blend until smooth.

• Makes 2 cups.

Tomato Cucumber Dip

A bit like a creamy salsa, this is good with chips of any kind.

1 small cucumber, peeled, seeded, chopped
3 slices crisp bacon, crumbled
1 ripe tomato, chopped
2 green onions, diced fine
3/4 cup sour cream
1 teaspoon lemon peel, grated
1 teaspoon fresh lemon juice
1 tablespoon fresh dill, chopped, or 2 teaspoons dry
1/8 teaspoon garlic powder

• Combine ingredients and mix, then refrigerate for an hour or more before serving.

• Makes about 1 2/3 cups.

Un-Clam Dip

Why would you want a clam dip without clams? Maybe you're allergic, or maybe a party happens spontaneously down the hall from your apartment and you don't have a clam in the house. Maybe you have guests coming who don't eat meat or seafood. Whatever the reason, this clam dip without clams tastes pretty darned good with veggies or crackers. Try it with buttered, toasted pita bread wedges, too. This is also perfect with a variety of fresh, raw vegetables, like zucchini slices, cucumber wedges, celery, carrots, etc.

1 cup sour cream
1 3 1/2-ounce package cream cheese, softened
1 8-10 ounce can whole kernel corn, drained
1 medium sweet red or green bell pepper, diced
1 green spring onion, diced
1/4 teaspoon dry mustard
1/8 teaspoon hot sauce
1 tablespoon soy sauce
2 teaspoons Worcestershire sauce
1/8 teaspoon Old Bay seasoning

• Mix sour cream and cream cheese in food processor until smooth. Add remaining ingredients and pulse blend until everything is lightly chopped but still chunky. Refrigerate for at least 2 hours for flavors to blend.

• Makes about 2 1/2 cups.

Watermelon Dip

A surprisingly different kind of party food, this is simple and very good. Surround the dip with cold, bite-sized watermelon pieces (with toothpicks) and honeydew pieces, too.

1 1/2 cups fresh lime juice
2 teaspoons any favorite hot sauce
1 teaspoon brown sugar
Salt to taste

• Mix ingredients and place in dipping bowl.

• Makes 1 1/2 cups.

Whiskey Barbecue Dipping Sauce

Serve this hot or cold, surrounded by your favorite buffalo wings.

1 cup catsup
1/4 cup whiskey
1/4 cup sorghum molasses
1/4 cup apple cider vinegar
Juice of 1/2 fresh lemon
1 tablespoon Worcestershire sauce
2 teaspoons hot sauce
1 tablespoon soy sauce
1/2 teaspoon black pepper
1/2 teaspoon dry mustard
1 clove garlic, minced

• Combine ingredients in saucepan and simmer for 10 minutes.

• Makes about 1 3/4 cups.

White Bean Dip

Serve with raw vegetables, cherry tomatoes or toasted pita bread pieces.

1 15-ounce can great northern beans, drained
1 clove garlic
1 tablespoon olive oil
Juice of 1/2 lemon
1/4 teaspoon ground cumin
1/2 cup picante sauce
1 green onion, diced fine

• Combine beans, garlic, olive oil, lemon juice and cumin in food processor and blend until smooth. Mix that with the picante sauce and top with the diced spring onion.

• Makes about 1 1/2 cups.

Yankee Beef Dip

Crackers or pita chips go best with this, but carrot or celery sticks also go well.

2 2 1/2-ounce jars dried beef, cut up
2 8-ounce packages cream cheese, softened
1/4 cup mayonnaise
1/2 cup sour cream
2 tablespoons milk or half and half
1 teaspoon Worcestershire sauce
Dash ground celery seed
2 green onions, diced

• Place beef in a food processor and pulse blend to chop the beef, then add remaining ingredients and pulse blend until well pulverized but not smooth. Serve chilled. For a hot dip, follow same directions then bake at 350° F. for 20 minutes.

• Makes about 2 1/2 cups.

Zucchini Dip

In summertime when you have more zucchini than you can give to neighbors, this is a good way to use up a bit more of the excess. It's an easy and good-for-you dip to serve with crackers or chips.

1 1/2 cups shredded zucchini
1 teaspoon salt
1 cup plain yogurt
2 tablespoons grated Parmesan cheese
2 teaspoons freshly squeezed lemon juice
1 clove garlic, minced, or 1/2 teaspoon garlic powder
10 fresh basil leaves, chopped fine, or 1 teaspoon dry
1/2 teaspoon grated lemon peel
Dash black pepper

• Mix salt and zucchini together and place in a strainer or colander. Set aside for 20 minutes to drain, then squeeze out most of the moisture. Combine zucchini with remaining ingredients in food processor and pulse blend, leaving the mixture coarse and a bit chunky. Refrigerate overnight.

• Makes about 2 1/2 cups.

Ethnic Dips

Possibly you'd like to add an exotic touch to your parties, or have a party with a theme. After trips I've taken to India, Thailand, Indonesia, etc., I have had friends over to see the souvenirs I've brought back from my travels. For those kinds of gatherings, I like to serve foods I have learned about in some of those exotic locations.

Aam Ka Sasam (South India)

This traditional south Indian mango dip can be served either chilled or at room temperature with warm chapatis or toasted pita bread pieces. (Chapatis are available frozen in Asian markets and can be toasted on a grill). If you don't have good, ripe mangoes, fresh pineapple can be used instead.

5 ripe mangoes, peeled, seeded
1/2 cup grated coconut,
  fresh if available
3-4 dried chilies, crushed
1 1/2 tablespoons brown sugar
1 teaspoon ground coriander
Dash salt

- Combine ingredients in food processor and pulse blend to chop. Refrigerate for 1-2 hours before serving.
- Makes about 3 1/2 cups.

Australian Dipping Sauce

Probably you could dip grilled kangaroo in this sauce, but given that most people won't have kangaroo on their party table, some sliced chicken or turkey will work just as well. Try this dip with grilled chicken wings or even lightly seasoned buffalo wings. You'll find lots of party foods to serve with this dipping sauce.

1 1/2 cups water
1 tablespoon sugar
2 tablespoons rice vinegar, or white wine vinegar
2 teaspoons fish sauce
1 dried hot pepper, crushed
1 tablespoon fresh ginger, grated
2 teaspoons soy sauce
6 lemon verbena or lemon basil leaves, chopped
2 teaspoons cornstarch, mixed with a little cold water

- Place everything in a nonstick skillet except for the cornstarch/water mixture. Simmer gently for a few minutes. While still simmering, stir in the cornstarch/water mixture and continue stirring until mixture thickens a bit.
- Makes about 1 3/4 cups.

What's lemon verbena?

It's a sweetly lemon flavored herb, a tree actually. It grows well in herb gardens as an annual, but in southern California or Florida, it will grow the year around and reach small tree size. It's botanical name is *Aloysia citriodora*, and can be found at lots of nurseries nationwide. The leaves dry or freeze well and can be used like fresh.

Baba Ghanouj, or Eggplant Dip (Middle Eastern)

This Middle Eastern dip is a traditional dip. Serve this with toasted pita bread triangles, crackers or fresh vegetables.

1 medium purple eggplant, about 1 pound
1 small onion, cut into pieces
1 clove garlic
1/4 cup fresh lemon juice
1 tablespoon olive or vegetable oil
1 1/2 teaspoons salt

• Pierce eggplant 3 or 4 times with fork and bake at 400° F. until very soft, about 30 minutes. Cool, then peel eggplant and cut into pieces. Combine all of the ingredients in food processor and blend until smooth. Serve at room temperature or slightly warmed.

• Makes about 2 cups.

Baba Ghanouj Dip #2 (Middle-Eastern)

Sometimes spelled ghanooj, this dip can be found in several countries and is often served with pita bread or other similar flat breads.

3 large eggplants
3/4 cup tahini (sesame seed paste)
1/2 cup lemon juice
2 cloves garlic, minced
1 teaspoon ground cumin
1/8 teaspoon cayenne pepper
Dash salt

For garnish:
2 tablespoons chopped black olives
1/4 cup chopped fresh parsley

• In the oven broiler, or on a barbecue grill, broil the eggplants, turning them often until the skins are blistered and blackened, about 20 minutes. Remove from oven and cool for a few minutes, then peel. Put the eggplant and remaining ingredients in a food processor and blend until smooth. Transfer into serving dish and garnish with chopped olives and parsley. To be truly authentic, drizzle some olive oil over the top after garnishing.

• Makes about 4-5 cups.

Bagna Cauda, Traditional (Northern Italy)

Pronounced bahn-ya caw-dah, *serve this warmed, as a dip for hearty toasted bread pieces, bread sticks or whole grain crackers. It's more like an oil dipping sauce than a traditional dip as we Westerners think of dips.*

3 2-ounce cans anchovy fillets, not drained
6 cloves garlic, minced
1 1/2 cups butter
3/4 cup olive oil
Juice of 1 lemon
2 teaspoons freshly ground black pepper

• Mince or chop the anchovies, saving some of the oil. Heat the butter in a saucepan and add the olive oil and lemon juice. Add anchovies and reserved oil, along with the garlic and black pepper and simmer briefly. Serve while still hot.

• Makes about 2 3/4 cups.

Bagna Cauda, Westernized Version

Bagna Cauda is a traditional northern Italian dip that is served hot, in cold weather. Generally served with fresh bread for dipping, I've adapted this to make a dip for bread sticks and fresh vegetables as well as Italian bread.

2 2-ounce cans anchovy fillets, drained except for 1 tablespoon oil
1 3 1/2-ounce package cream cheese, softened
1/4 cup mayonnaise
2 cloves garlic, crushed
2 tablespoons fresh parsley, chopped

• Combine ingredients in food processor and process until fairly smooth.

• Makes about 1/2 cup.

Banana Chutney (South Indian)

Serve this with toasted Indian flat bread, or pita bread, cut in pieces.

1-2 tablespoons vegetable oil
1 medium onion, chopped
2 green bananas, diced
2 tablespoons hot, red pepper, chopped
1/2 cup red wine
2 tablespoons brown sugar
2 teaspoons ground coriander
Dash salt

• Put oil in skillet and sauté onion until lightly browned. Add diced banana and stir, then add wine, sugar, red pepper, coriander and salt. Simmer for 3-4 minutes. Serve at room temperature.

• Makes about 3/4 cup.

Banana Raita
(from Gujarat, a state in western India)

South Indian food is notoriously hot and spicy and this dip is a cooling balance to those foods. Serve this dip with very hot, spicy buffalo wings or with other similar hot, spicy foods.

1 ripe banana, mashed
1 cup plain yogurt
1 tablespoon cilantro chopped fine
Dash salt

- Combine the ingredients and mix until smooth.
- Makes about 1 1/4 cups.

Butter Bean Dip (English)

Oh those inventive English! Who else would ever dream up a dip that's made out of butter beans? But this one's pretty good and contains no dairy products, yet is a pleasantly creamy dip. If you want to avoid a lot of sour cream and cheese products, put this on your party table and let people guess what it's made of. Crackers, chips and raw vegetable sticks are perfect with this. I've adapted it to be, well, more American and not quite so stiff-upper-lippishly English.

2 small zucchinis, cut in pieces
1 garlic clove, minced
2 16-ounce cans of butter beans, drained
2 tablespoons grated Parmesan cheese
2 tablespoons fresh basil, chopped
Salt and black pepper
1/8 teaspoon hot sauce

- Place the zucchini pieces and garlic in microwave-safe container, covered, and microwave on high for about 8 minutes or until the zucchini is tender. Drain and place in a food processor with remaining ingredients and process until smooth. Let flavors combine for an hour or more before serving. Serve warm or chilled.
- Makes about 2 1/4 cups.

Cacik (Turkey)

This is a traditional Turkish dip, somewhat like Tzatziki, listed elsewhere alphabetically in the ethnic dips. Serve this chilled, with pita bread pieces.

1 1/2 cups yogurt
2 cloves garlic, crushed
2 medium cucumbers,
  peeled, seeded, grated
1/2 teaspoon salt
1/8 cup chopped fresh mint
2 tablespoons olive oil
1/8 teaspoon crushed sumac berries

- Press the shredded cucumber between paper towels to remove excess moisture. Combine the cucumber with the yogurt, salt, garlic and mint and mix. Then stir in the olive oil and top with crushed sumac berries.
- Makes about 1 3/4 cups.

What are sumac berries?

Botanically it's *Rhus glabra*, although several varieties are used. The berries are sour, a bit lemony. In the U.S., sumac grows wild from Texas to Ohio and beyond, and is sometimes used for a lemonade-like beverage, or jelly making. In the Middle East, sumac berries are a traditional seasoning herb and in India the berries are used to aid digestion. In the Ozarks, sumac berries are used for a cooling drink much like lemonade in late summer. It can be found in ethnic groceries and by mail order. (Remember: pronounce sugar, sumac and sure "sh".)

Caponata (Italy)

Serve with toasted Italian bread pieces, bread sticks, or your favorite crackers.

1 large eggplant
Juice of 1/2 lemon
2 teaspoons salt
3/4 cup olive oil, divided
1 cup diced onion
1 cup diced celery
1 cup diced red bell pepper
2 cups canned tomatoes
1/2 cup chopped green olives
3 tablespoons sugar
1/4 cup tomato sauce
2 cloves garlic, minced
1/2 cup red wine vinegar
2 teaspoons anchovy paste
Salt and black pepper
2 tablespoons capers
1/4 cup black olives, chopped

- Coarsely dice the unpeeled eggplant and sprinkle with lemon juice and salt. Set aside in a colander for the salt to draw out the moisture. Rinse, then squeeze most of the moisture out of the eggplant and drain on paper towel. Pour half of the 3/4 cup olive oil into a skillet, heated to medium. Add the diced onion and sauté until transparent but not browned. Add celery and pepper and cook on medium heat, stirring occasionally, about 10 minutes. Pour out into a bowl and set aside. Add remaining half of olive oil in skillet and add the eggplant, cooking and stirring frequently, until lightly browned. Add back the onion/celery/bell pepper mixture, along with the tomatoes, tomato sauce, anchovy paste, olives, sugar and vinegar. and simmer for about 20 minutes. Remove from heat and stir in the capers and cool. Right before serving, stir in the black olives.
- Makes about 6 cups.

Caponata #2

Serve with French bread or crackers.

1 large eggplant, diced
3 tablespoons olive oil
1 16-ounce can diced tomatoes
1/4 cup chopped black olives
2 cloves garlic, minced
1 teaspoon dry basil
1/2 teaspoon dry oregano,
  or 1 teaspoon fresh
Juice of 1/2 fresh lemon

• Heat oil in skillet and cook the eggplant, stirring frequently until soft. Add tomatoes, olives, lemon juice and garlic, reduce heat to low, cover with a lid and simmer for about 20 minutes, adding water if needed to keep from sticking. Mix in basil, oregano, salt and pepper. Serve at room temperature.

• Makes about 3 cups.

Capunatina (Italy)

Translated, it means, "the little caponata," like a mini-version of caponata, the traditional Italian dip or spread. This dip is easy, and a simplified version of the old favorite. Serve it with toasted pita pieces or toasted Italian bread. In Europe, eggplant is known as aubergine.

1 purple eggplant, peeled, cubed
1 tablespoon salt
4 ripe Roma tomatoes, diced
4 red or yellow bell peppers,
  seeded, diced
1/3 cup grated provolone cheese
1 medium onion, coarsely diced
2 cloves garlic, minced
Olive oil
Dash salt and black pepper
2 teaspoons fresh,
  or 1 teaspoon dry basil
1/2 cup white wine

• Preheat the oven to 375° F. Toss the eggplant cubes with salt, place in a colander and let drain for about an hour. Rinse the eggplant and dry on paper towels, then combine that with the other ingredients, except the wine, in a baking dish. Sprinkle liberally with olive oil, then salt, pepper and basil, and bake for 30 minutes. Stir in the half cup wine, and bake another 30 minutes. Serve warm.

• Makes about 5 cups.

Cheese Fondue (Switzerland)

This is a classic Swiss fondue and is traditionally served in a fondue pot, with crusty French bread that's been cut into pieces, each having a bit of crust. Use fondue forks for dipping the bread into the hot cheese dip.

1 medium clove garlic
2 cups dry white wine
1 pound shredded Swiss cheese
1 teaspoon cornstarch
3 tablespoons kirsch or brandy
Tiny pinch ground nutmeg
1/8 teaspoon hot sauce

• Rub the inside of the fondue pot with the garlic clove. Pour in wine and place over low heat. When air bubbles begin to rise to the surface, add the shredded cheese. Stir until cheese is melted. Dissolve cornstarch in the kirsch or brandy; add to cheese fondue mixture, and continue cooking, stirring for another 2-3 minutes. Place over alcohol burner and it's ready to serve. Mix in nutmeg and hot sauce.

• Makes about 3 cups.

Chili Garlic Peanut Dip (Thailand)

Cucumber slices, cheese wedges and bagel chips all go well with this traditional dip, but grilled chicken wings or turkey slices, also taste great with this. I learned to make this while in Bangkok one January at the Boipai Cooking School.

4 cloves garlic
3 dried red chilies
1 cup dry roasted, salted peanuts
1/4 cup plain yogurt

• Combine garlic and chilies in food processors and pulse blend. Pour into mixing bowl, then grind the peanuts to a powder and add to the garlic and chilies, and mix in the yogurt.

• Makes about 1 1/3 cups.

Chili-Tomato Dip (Thailand)

Known as nam Prik Num in Thailand, this is a traditional dipping sauce for fresh vegetables or chips. It also serves well as a condiment with rice dishes. It will keep several days in the refrigerator and is even better if made the day before serving. I've reduced the amount of fish sauce for American tastes but if you want it to be authentic, increase the fish sauce to 3 tablespoons.

2 large banana chilies
or yellow hot wax chilies
2 shallots, peeled, cut in half
5 cloves garlic, peeled
2 medium sized, ripe tomatoes
1 tablespoon fresh cilantro
1 tablespoon fish sauce
Juice of 1 fresh lime

• Roast the peppers by "dry frying," which is to heat a skillet to high heat and add the whole peppers, without any oil. Push down with a spoon or spatula and turn occasionally, about 5 minutes or until the skins are blackened and charred. Remove the peppers and do the same with the tomatoes, roasting until the skins are blackened, then cool. Remove the stems and seeds from the peppers but do not remove the skins. Cut the tomatoes in pieces. Place peppers, tomatoes, shallots and garlic in food processor and coarsely chop. Put the mixture into a small bowl, stir in the cilantro, fish sauce and lime juice and mix.

• Makes about 1 1/4 cups.

Cucumber Dip (Greece)

This is also know as Tsatsiki or Tzatziki and is good for dipping dolmas (stuffed grape leaves, a Greek delicacy) as well as for dipping toasted pita bread triangles, raw vegetables, crackers, etc.

1 large cucumber, peeled, seeded, diced
1 teaspoon salt
2 cups plain yogurt
8 green onions, finely chopped
2 cloves garlic, minced
1/4 cup freshly chopped mint
Dash salt and pepper

• Salt the diced cucumber generously and place in a colander to drain for about 30 minutes, then rinse and dry on paper towel. Beat together the yogurt in a bowl with the garlic, green onion, salt and pepper, then mix in the chopped mint, then add that to the cucumber. Top with more freshly chopped mint. Chill for at least an hour before serving.

• Makes about 2 3/4 cups.

Cucumber Mint Dip (India)

Many dips from India are used to balance the hot and spicy seasonings of the food, especially in South India. This is a simple dip, somewhat thin like a sauce and quick to make. It's very good served with hot and spicy chicken wings and is especially good in summer as cucumber is a cooling vegetable. Serve it with toasted roti (also known as chapatti) or paratha bread.

2 cups plain yogurt
1 1/2 cups finely shredded cucumber
2 teaspoons salt
2 tablespoons freshly chopped mint leaves

- Combine salt and cucumber and mix, then set aside to let the salt draw out some of the moisture. Rinse and combine with the yogurt and mint, mixing well. Refrigerate until ready to serve.
- Makes about 3 1/3 cups.

What's a chapati?

Chapati, also spelled chapatti are flat breads similar to parathas and puris, each made slightly differently in different parts of India. The word chapati is not Indian, the locals call it roti. It is made from whole grain durum wheat flour called atta flour, water and salt by rolling the dough out into discs of approximately 6 or 8 inches in diameter and browning it on both sides on a hot, dry griddle. Each chapati is then held for about a second over an open flame, causing it to puff up with steam like a balloon.

Curry Dip (English)

Curry seasoning is an English invention, rather than an Indian mixture and while Westerners can find curry seasoning in the spice section of the grocery store (and believe they are eating authentic Indian seasoning), Indians would not recognize the seasoning at all for cooking. The English, while they occupied India, tried to imitate the masala seasoning blends that Indians use in their cooking. "Curry" powder is that English imitation of the real thing. This uses the non-Indian, English/American curry seasoning from the grocery store. Use as a dip for raw vegetables or chips. It's very tasty!

1 cup plain yogurt
1/2 cups mayonnaise
2 teaspoons curry powder
1 tablespoon grated onion
1/2 teaspoon dry mustard
1/8 teaspoon hot sauce
1 teaspoon fresh lemon juice
Dash salt and pepper

• Combine ingredients and mix. Chill an hour or longer before serving.

• Makes 1 1/2 cups.

Curried Cucumber Dip (Canadian)

Serve this with lots of celery and carrot sticks, apple wedges and crackers. It's also good served with toasted paratha pieces.

1 cup mayonnaise
1/2 cup plain yogurt
2 medium cucumbers, peeled, seeded, shredded
1/4 cup finely grated carrot
1/4 cup roasted, chopped pecans or almonds
1 tablespoon frozen orange juice concentrate
1/8 teaspoon, or more, curry powder

• Combine ingredients, mixing well. Refrigerate until ready to serve.

• Makes about 3 cups.

Dahi Chutney Dip (Northern India)

Mughalai food has its origins in the royal banquets of the Mogul Empire period of Indian history. Barbecued meats that had been slowly cooked over the fire, accompanied by spicy dals and other royal dishes, were the tradition with this dip. Served now with dosas, idilis, puris or just plain toasted pita bread triangles, this is a very traditional Indian dip. (Dahi is the Hindi word for yogurt). This makes a fairly tart, spicy, but cooling dip to serve with hotter, spicier foods. Try it with spicy buffalo wings. Toasted paratha pieces go well with this, too.

2 cups plain yogurt
1 cup chopped cilantro
5 green chilies or jalapenos, chopped fine
1/2 teaspoon *roasted cumin seeds, ground
1 clove garlic, minced fine, or 1 teaspoon garlic powder
1 teaspoon fresh lemon juice
Dash salt

* Cumin seeds are roasted in a hot pan without oil, for about a minute, stirring, before grinding. The roasting changes the flavor considerably, so don't skip this step, then grind them in a blender.

• Mix ingredients together and refrigerate. Serve cold.

• Makes about 3 cups.

Mughals were indian rulers who originally came from Afghanistan. Their cuisine, Mughalai cuisine, was a mix of Persian and Mongolian. (Mongolian because the mother of the first Mughal king, Babur was a Mongol; and the use of yogurt and cream in curries is typically Mongolian and the use of barbecued meats is typical of Persian cuisine, and the spices are typical of Indian dishes).

Use of milk, yogurt and cream in curries and dips is very typical of the mughalai cuisine. Most Indian restaurants in the U.S. use this cuisine as it is more accepted and popular in the West, according to Puneet Sharma, New Delhi/Washington, D.C.

Dhaniya Chutney, or Cilantro Dip (Northern India)

Also from my friend, Puneet Sharma, this can be served as a dip for grilled buffalo/chicken wings or as a dipping sauce for barbecued or grilled meats or toasted paratha or pita bread.

2 cups plain yogurt
1 1/2 cups loosely packed coriander leaves
3 green chilies or jalapenos, stems removed
1/2 teaspoon roasted, then ground, cumin seeds
2 cloves garlic
1 teaspoon fresh lemon juice
Dash salt and black pepper

- Combine ingredients in a food processor and blend until smooth.
- Makes about 3 cups.

What is a paratha?

Parathas are somewhat like chapattis and puris, but fried in ghee (clarified butter) and often stuffed with vegetable dishes. They can be cut into pieces and toasted for dippers.

Ginger Dipping Sauce (Cambodian)

Known in Cambodia as Tirk khngay, this can be served as a dip for cold fish, chicken nuggets, chicken/buffalo wings, cubes of turkey on toothpicks. Note, the original recipe called for 1/8 cup fish sauce instead of the 1-2 tablespoons listed here; to be traditional, you can use the original amount, but most Westerners don't like that much fish sauce. Add more to taste.

1/8 cup fresh lime juice
1/8 cup hot water
1/8 cup brown sugar
1-2 tablespoons fish sauce
2 tablespoons grated ginger
2 garlic cloves, minced

• Combine juice, hot water and brown sugar and stir until sugar is dissolved. Add remaining ingredients and leave at room temperature until ready to serve.

• Makes about 1/2 cup.

Goat Cheese & Pepper Dip (Spain)

This is an excellent dip for serving with crackers, bagel slices or raw vegetables.

1/2 cup canned, roasted sweet peppers, drained
2 green onions, diced
1 tablespoon capers, drained
1 clove garlic
12 ounces fresh goat cheese
1 teaspoon Dijon mustard
2 tablespoons olive oil
Dash any favorite hot sauce
Dash black pepper

• Place peppers, onions, capers and garlic in food processor and blend until smooth. Add remaining ingredients and blend well. Chill before serving.

• Makes about 2 cups.

Hot Tomato Dip (India)

This is a delicious dipping sauce for warm chapatis torn into pieces, or lightly buttered and toasted pita bread, cut into wedges.

1 teaspoon cumin seed
3 tablespoons vegetable oil
4 ripe tomatoes, chopped
2 cloves garlic, diced
2 green chilies such as seranno, seeded, diced
2 teaspoons brown sugar
1-2 teaspoons chili powder
Dash salt and pepper

• Heat oil in skillet and add cumin seeds and toast, about 1 minute. Add garlic and sauté until lightly browned. Add chopped tomatoes and green chilies. Cook for about 2 minutes, stirring, then add remaining ingredients. Serve warm.

• Makes about 1 1/4 cups.

Hummus Dip (Middle Eastern)

Toasted pita bread triangles go well with this dip. Garbanzo beans are also known as chick peas.

1 15 1/2-ounce can garbanzo beans
1/4 cup chopped onion
Juice of one freshly squeezed lemon
1 clove garlic
1 teaspoon fresh basil or 1/2 teaspoon dried
1/2 teaspoon hot sauce

• Drain the garbanzos, except for 1/4 cup liquid. Combine all ingredients in food processor and process until smooth. Refrigerate for an hour or more for flavors to blend.

• Makes about 1 1/4 cups.

Hummus, Tuscan Style

10 garlic cloves
2 15-ounce cans great northern or cannellini beans, drained, juice reserved
1/2 cup tahini (sesame paste)
Juice of 3 lemons
1 tablespoon soy sauce
1/2 teaspoon cayenne pepper
1/8 teaspoon ground coriander
1 teaspoon ground cumin

• In a food processor, chop the garlic then add the beans and chop. Combine the rest of the ingredients and blend until smooth. If too thick, add a bit of the reserved bean juice (if not needed, discard the juice). Scrape into a serving bowl and refrigerate, then top with tomato topping, below.

• Makes about 3 1/2 cups.

Tomato Topping for Hummus:

4 ripe Roma tomatoes, seeded, diced
1 garlic clove, minced
1 tablespoon freshly chopped basil
1/8 cup olive oil
Dash salt
1 tablespoon freshly chopped parsley

• Combine ingredients except parsley, tossing well, and refrigerate. To serve the humus, surround it with toasted pita bread pieces and top the hummus with the Tomato Topping, adding the chopped parsley on top.

Hummus (Mexico)

A zippier version of this much loved bean dip. If you like it hot, add another jalapeno to the recipe.

1 15-ounce can garbanzo beans, drained, juice reserved
1 fresh jalapeno, with or without the seeds, diced
1/2 teaspoon cumin or substitute taco seasoning
Juice of 1 lemon
3 cloves garlic
Dash salt
2-3 tablespoons freshly chopped cilantro, divided
1 tablespoon freshly chopped parsley

- Combine everything except cilantro and parsley in food processor and blend until smooth. If too thick, add a bit of the reserved juice from the garbanzos and blend again (otherwise, discard the juice). Stir in the cilantro, scrape into serving dish, top with chopped cilantro and parsley and cover and refrigerate until ready to serve.
- Makes about 1 1/4 cups.

Note: Leaving the seeds in the pepper make for a hotter hummus. It's not the seed, but rather the membrane around the seed, where the most heat is in a pepper. However, removing the seeds, also removes most of the membrane. Also, an optional ingredient to add if you have it handy, is half a roasted red sweet pepper, which gives a nice added flavor to this recipe.

Kiwifruit Dip (Australia)

Surround a dip bowl of this with cubed honeydew, cantaloupe, jicama, strawberries and grapes. Also goes well with hot and spicy buffalo wings.

3 kiwis, peeled, quartered
1 teaspoon freshly grated ginger
3 tablespoons olive or light vegetable oil
Juice of 1 lime
2 teaspoons honey
Dash cayenne pepper
Salt and pepper

• Combine all the ingredients in a food processor and blend until very smooth.

Lemon Balm & Orange Dip (Australia)

Serve this with hot and spicy buffalo wings, or grilled chicken wings. It also goes well with cubes of honeydew and cantaloupe, or grapes, strawberries or other fruit.

4 tablespoons chopped fresh lemon balm leaves
3 oranges, peeled, seeded, diced
2 teaspoons fresh lemon juice
1 cup plain yogurt
2 teaspoons honey or sugar
1/8 teaspoon cayenne pepper
Salt, to taste, optional

• Combine ingredients in food processor and blend until fairly smooth, leaving flecks of lemon balm. Refrigerate for 30 minutes or more and serve.

• Makes about 1 3/4 cups.

What is Lemon Balm?

Lemon balm, (*Melissa officinalis*) is a perennial herb with a pleasantly lemony flavor. Like most herbs, the best flavor comes from the newest growth. The more you harvest it, the faster it grows and the better the flavor. Older lemon balm, going to flower or seed, will not have the best flavor, in fact, may taste a bit "soapy."

Mango-Peanut Dip (Gujrat, western India)

Serve with pita bread (toasted or plain), chapatti, roasted meats, buffalo wings or grilled chicken wings.

2 cups coriander leaves
3 green chilies or jalapenos
1/2 teaspoon *roasted cumin seeds
3 heaping tablespoons peanut butter
1 teaspoon fresh lemon juice
1 mango (choose a very sour variety of mango)
Dash salt
Pinch of black pepper or chili pepper, optional

*To roast cumin seed, place them in a medium-hot skillet and shake or stir until they give up their pleasant aroma. Cool, then grind in blender.

• Combine all the ingredients in food processor and pulse blend until well chopped.

• Makes about 1 1/3 cups.

Nam Prik Kiga (Thailand)

A traditional Thai dip for barbecued meats. Serve it with cold, sliced turkey, chicken or pork, or with barbecued chicken wings.

1 tablespoon oil
6 tablespoons fresh green birds eye chilies, crushed
6 tablespoons fresh or dry red birds eye chilies, crushed
2 shallots, thinly sliced
2 garlic cloves, diced
3 tablespoons fresh cilantro, chopped
Juice of 1 fresh lime
1 tablespoon (or less) fish sauce

• Heat oil in a skillet and add the chilies, shallots and garlic and sauté just until cooked but not browned. Remove from heat, cool briefly and transfer to a food processor with remaining ingredients and blend until you have a smooth paste.

• Makes about 1/2 cup.

Peanut Dipping Sauce (Thailand)

Serve this dip with slices of roasted duck, chicken or turkey. It's a traditional dipping sauce in Thailand to serve with grilled satay, and is good with any grilled meats.

1 cup dry roasted, unsalted peanuts
1/2 cup green onion, chopped
2 cloves garlic, minced
1/2 cup coconut milk
2 tablespoons water
1 teaspoon soy sauce
1 teaspoon fresh lime juice
1/2 teaspoon brown sugar
1/2 teaspoon fresh ginger, grated
1/2 teaspoon ground coriander
1/4 teaspoon crushed dry red pepper

- Put ingredients in food processor or blender and blend until you have a paste. Slowly simmer over low heat, stirring, about 10 minutes. Thin with a bit of water or coconut milk if desired.
- Makes about 1 cup.

Persian Cucumber Dip (Iran)

Serve this traditional dip with toasted pita bread pieces or grilled chicken wings.

1 cup plain yogurt
1 small onion, cut in pieces
1 cucumber, peeled, seeded
1/4 cup raisins
1/4 cup chopped fresh mint
Dash salt

- Combine ingredients in food processor and pulse blend until everything is coarsely chopped. Refrigerate for a few hours to let flavors blend.
- Makes about 2 cups.

Persian Cucumber Dip, Traditional (Iran)

Called Must-o-Khiar, this is the more traditional version of the slightly Americanized dip, above. Pita chips, toasted pita bread or crackers go well with this.

2 cups plain yogurt
2 small cucumbers, peeled, seeded
1/4 cup golden raisins
2 tablespoons walnuts
2 tablespoons chopped fresh mint, or 1 tablespoon dry
Dash salt and pepper

• Combine ingredients in food processor and pulse blend just enough to coarsely chop everything. Refrigerate a few hours before serving.

• Makes about 2 3/4 cups.

Pudina Chutney - Mint Dip (Northern India)

Chutneys are often served as a side dish, like we would serve a relish, to accompany meats or vegetable dishes. Chutneys are also eaten by dipping with torn chapati bread, or toasted pita bread pieces, and this also goes well with tandori chicken, or any kind of baked, barbecued or broiled chicken wings. This recipe comes from my friend, Puneet Sharma, who grew up in New Delhi, India.

2 cups plain yogurt
1 1/2 cups chopped fresh coriander
3 green chilies or jalapenos, seeded
1/2 teaspoon *roasted cumin seeds
2 cups chopped fresh mint
1 teaspoon fresh lemon juice
Dash salt
Pinch of black pepper or cayenne, optional

*To roast cumin seed, place them in a medium-hot skillet and shake or stir until they give up their pleasant aroma, about 1 minute. Cool, then grind in blender or food processor.

• Combine ingredients in food processor and process to a smooth consistency.

• Makes about 3 cups.

Salmorejo (Spanish)

Although this is sometimes described as being a bit like a gazpacho, this is a milder version and unique to the south of Spain, specifically, I am told, to the areas around Cordoba. Serve this with hearty pieces of French or Italian bread, or with toasted pita wedges. It's a bit bland but it would also go with very spicy barbecued chicken wings. Or add a bit of parsley and fresh oregano, but then you have Italian instead of Spanish!

3 ripe tomatoes, quartered, seeded
2 tablespoons olive oil
1 clove garlic
1/2 teaspoon salt
3 slices white or Italian bread, torn in pieces

• Place tomatoes in blender, and with blender running on low, drizzle in the olive oil, then add the garlic and salt; then add the torn bread pieces to the tomato mixture and blend into a sauce. If too thin, add another half slice of bread and blend until smooth. Refrigerate for an hour before serving.

• Makes about 2 1/2 cups.

Spanish Dip

Make this ahead of time and refrigerate for a day or two. The flavor improves with age. Serve with crackers, chips or toasted bread pieces.

1/4 cup chopped black olives
1/4 cup canned chopped green chilies
1 onion, chopped fine
3 tomatoes, chopped
3 tablespoons olive oil
2 tablespoons red wine vinegar
Dash salt and pepper
1 teaspoon fresh lemon juice

• Mix together and refrigerate overnight before serving.

• Makes about 2 1/2 cups.

Spicy Vinegar Dipping Sauce (Korea)

This is a traditional Korean dipping sauce for grilled beef, seafood or lightly grilled vegetables.

1 cup rice vinegar
1/2 cup soy sauce
1/4 cup sugar
2 teaspoons sesame oil
(dark if available)
1 1/2 tablespoons freshly
grated ginger
2 cloves garlic, minced
2 green onions, finely diced
1 dry chili pod, crushed or
1 teaspoon cayenne
2 teaspoons sesame seeds, *toasted

*Toast sesame seeds in a hot skillet, stirring or tossing for about 1 minute.

• Combine vinegar, soy sauce and sugar stirring until sugar is dissolved. Add remaining ingredients except sesame seeds and set aside for 1 hour. Before serving, sprinkle the sesame seeds on top.

• Makes about 2 cups.

Tapanade (South France)

Tapanade is a black olive spread or dip and always includes olive oil, combined with a mixture of anchovies, capers, herbs and garlic. Serve with toasted French bread pieces or buttered, toasted pita bread wedges.

3 ounces *reconstituted
sun dried tomatoes
1/2 cup pitted and
chopped green olives
1 teaspoon anchovy paste,
or 1 anchovy, rinsed
3 tablespoons extra virgin olive oil
2 garlic cloves
1/2 teaspoon dry marjoram
or 1 teaspoon fresh
Dash freshly ground black pepper

*To reconstitute sun dried tomatoes, soak in 1 or 2 tablespoons sherry vinegar, or warm water. until soft, about 10 minutes.

• Combine tomatoes, olives and anchovy paste in food processor and pulse blend. Add olive oil and process until fairly smooth, then add pepper.

• Makes about 3/4 cup.

Teriyaki Dipping Sauce (Japan)

Serve this dip with grilled or baked chicken or pork slices. It also works well as a marinade for grilling.

1/2 cup brown sugar
1/2 cup rice wine (sake)
1 clove garlic, crushed
1 teaspoon fresh lemon juice
1/2 teaspoon grated lemon peel
1/2 teaspoon freshly grated ginger

• Mix ingredients and serve at room temperature.

• Makes 1 cup.

Tamatar Chutney, or Tomato Dip (Northern India)

The word chutney is a British version of the Indian word, chatni. This recipe comes from my friend, Puneet Sharma, who grew up in New Delhi. Northern Indian food is completely different from Southern Indian food, as I learned when I traveled there. Serve this with toasted pita bread or chapatis that are warmed and torn into pieces. This also is good served with party crackers.

2 teaspoons whole cumin seed
1 tablespoon oil
3 medium tomatoes, peeled. diced
4 tablespoons brown sugar
Juice of 1 lemon
3 jalapenos, seeded, chopped
Salt to taste
Dash paprika
1 cup cilantro, chopped

• Heat oil in pan, add cumin and wait until it pops and changes flavor. Add peppers and sauté until soft, then add tomatoes, brown sugar and lemon juice, cover and simmer for flavors to combine, about 3 minutes. Add paprika and salt, mixing. Remove from heat and cool briefly, then garnish with cilantro leaves and serve while still warm.

• Makes about 1 1/2 cups.

Tzatziki (Greece)

A traditional Greek dip, served with pita bread. Tzatziki is both a Greek and Turkish meze, or appetizer, also used as a sauce or dip. The Greek word came from the Turkish word, cacık, which means a form of chutney. It is always made from yogurt, which was traditionally made from sheep or goat milk. Often dill or mint is added to tzatziki, and Turkish kebabs as well as Greek gyros are also served with this dip. In Iran this dish is known as djadjik. In India, the dip would be called raita, and served like an appetizer with other dishes. In the Caucasus mountains, kaffir instead of yogurt is used, and it's turned into a cooling summer drink, which points out what a widespread recipe this is.

1 large cucumber, peeled, seeded, shredded
4 garlic cloves, minced
Dash salt and pepper
2 teaspoons fresh lemon juice
1 cup plain yogurt
1 tablespoon olive oil
1 tablespoon finely chopped fresh mint

• Drain grated cucumber in colander, or press between paper towels to remove excess juice, then mix with remaining ingredients and refrigerate until ready to serve.

• Makes about 2 cups.

Tzatziki, Simple Version (Greek-American)

2 medium cucumbers, peeled, seeded, grated
1 1/2 cups Greek-style yogurt
5 cloves garlic, minced
Dash salt
1/2 teaspoon white wine vinegar
1 tablespoon olive oil

• Press the grated cucumber between paper towels to remove excess juice. Mix cucumber with yogurt, garlic, salt and vinegar, then add olive oil, mixing well.

• Makes about 2 1/2 cups.

Won Ton Dipping Sauce (Chinese)

My Chinese chef friend, Eddie Chong, from Malaysia, taught me to make this outstanding sauce at the same time he taught me how to make won tons. The dip is traditional for serving with won tons, and makes a great party food or one course of a bigger meal.

1 large onion, cut in chunks
4-6 medium-to-hot, fresh red peppers, such as seranno or jalapeno, seeds removed
4 cloves garlic, peeled
4 tablespoons oil
1/2 cup soy sauce
1 cup rice vinegar or white wine vinegar
3 tablespoons brown sugar

• Combine onion, peppers and garlic in food processor and chop to a medium-fine consistency. Heat oil in skillet on low heat and add the vegetables from the food processor. Stir, continuing to cook on low heat until the oil takes on the color of the peppers. You'll notice as you stir that the peppers will change colors, darkening a bit and the fragrance will be less onion, and more of a tasty-smelling blend. In a bowl, pour the vinegar, soy sauce and brown sugar and stir to dissolve the sugar. Taste the mixture, it should be salty, slightly sweet and a bit sour. If too sour, add some more sugar. Mix, then add the mixture from the skillet. Serve warm or at room temperature with freshly steamed or fried won tons.

• Makes about 2 1/4 cups.

To blanch vegetables for dippers:

Prepare a pan of water in advance with lots of ice cubes and set aside. Bring water to boil in a pan. As soon as the water is bubbling, drop in the vegetables. For cauliflower or broccoli, give it about 1 minute in the boiling water. For asparagus, snow peas or other light vegetables, leave them in the boiling water about 30 seconds. Remove the vegetables from the boiling water and drop them immediately into the iced water to stop the cooking. Leave for 1-2 minutes, drain well and refrigerate until ready to serve.

Serving tips:

- *Hollow out a loaf of French bread and fill it with dip.*
- *Hollow out the top and insides of a round artisan bread and use that as a dipping bowl.*
- *Use a large bell pepper as a dip serving bowl.*
- *Empty out the insides of a small melon and fill with cubed fruit and set a bowl of dip in the middle or at the side.*
- *Make a dip serving bowl out of a hollowed out head of cabbage.*
- *Grapefruit, raw squash, a head of lettuce, small melons, large squash, all can be used for interesting dip serving bowls.*

Roasting Peppers

Make your own roasted peppers for dips. Any peppers can be roasted, and the flavor will be different, sweeter with a more "nutty" flavor, than the fresh pepper. Sweet bell peppers roast just fine, as do jalapenos, serannos, cayennes, Hungarian wax or any favorite pepper.

Either directly under the broiler in the oven, or on a hot barbecue grill, lay out the peppers you want to roast. Char them completely, until the skin is black and peeling, then turn the pepper and continue charring all of the sides of the peppers. With tongs, remove the peppers and drop them into a paper bag (paper works better than plastic for this).

Close up the bag and leave the peppers to steam in the bag for about 10 minutes. Remove when cool enough to handle and the peelings can easily be removed and discarded. Remove the stems and seed from the peppers and they are ready to use in a dip, or frozen for later use. Roasted peppers are great for all kinds of uses, including dips, in soup, in salad dressings, or just as a topping on grilled steak or chicken.

Quick "roasted" peppers:

When in a hurry and you need roasted peppers for a recipe, use this shortcut. Remove the stem and seed of the pepper you are going to use in the recipe. Chop it in a food processor until finely chopped. Put a tiny bit of oil in a skillet, heat to low-medium, and fry the peppers, stirring constantly. In about 10 minutes the peppers will change flavor to more like roasted peppers.

Another pepper roasting method I learned from a television host, who visited me: Use a cast iron griddle or similar skillet and heat it to medium-hot. Lay the peppers you will use in the recipe on the griddle and char them on all sides, 10-15 minutes. Be sure to keep them on the griddle until they are blackened on all sides. Judith doesn't peel the peppers when using this method, she just removes the stems and seeds then proceeds with the rest of the recipe and the flavor is outstanding!

Making Tahini

If you don't have access to tahini, you can make your own. Toast sesame seeds in a medium-hot skillet, shaking or stirring often, about 3 minutes until they are a golden brown. Cool the seeds then grind them to a paste in a blender with a bit of olive oil. Store in refrigerator until ready to use.

Things to dip:

- Apricot halves (dried or fresh)
- Apple wedges dipped in lemon juice to prevent browning
- Asparagus, raw or blanched
- Bagel bites
- Beef cubes or slices
- Broccoli
- Cabbage leaf ribs
- Carrots
- Cauliflower
- Celery
- Chicken nuggets
- Cucumber slices
- Endive
- Green onions
- Red or green bell pepper strips
- Jicama sticks
- Sliced cold turkey
- Chicken
- Chips
- Pita bread triangles (toasted or plain)
- Chapati bread pieces Toasted or plain
- Radishes
- Shrimp
- Snow peas (raw or blanched)
- Pears
- Firm cheese sticks
- Turnip slices
- French fries
- Fried onion rings
- Steamed artichoke petals
- Lightly steamed cardoon stems
- Blanched but crisp green beans
- Banana bites
- Fresh pineapple spears
- Melon pieces
- Whole strawberries
- Blueberries on a pick
- Grapes
- Cherry tomatoes
- Cauliflower or broccoli pieces
- Toasted tortilla pieces
- Toasted paratha bread
- Crackers
- Rye toast, breadsticks
- Fried won ton wrappers
- Whole baby mushrooms
- Endive center ribs
- Grilled chicken wings
- Grilled pork ribs
- Lamb riblets
- Stuffed shrimp
- Zucchini wedges

INDEX

Ethnic Dips

Sidebars:

Sources

Want to know more about Jim Long's other books and products?
Visit www.Longcreekherbs.com for a tour through his beautiful garden, or to browse in the shop. There is a blog containing many of Jim's columns, a way to send free e-postcards to your friends, plus much, much more!

For those who would like to grow their own fresh herbs, we recommend these excellent sources:

Baker Creek Heirloom Seed
2728 Baker Creek Rd.
Mansfield, MO 65704
417-924-8917
www.Rareseed.com

Mountain Valley Growers
38325 Pepperweed Rd.
Squaw Valley, CA 93675
www.mountainvalleygrowers.com

Nichols Garden Nursery
1190 Old Salem Rd, NE
Albany, OR 97321
800-422-3985
www.nicholsgardennursery.com

Papa Geno's Herb Farm
& Prairie Home Perennials
5835 West Roca Road
Martell, NE 68404
402-794-0400
www.papagenos.com

Richters Herbs
Goodwood, Ontario LOC 1A0, Canada
1-905-640-6677
www.Richter.com

Notes

Notes

Notes

Notes